BARRON'S BOOK NOTES

UPTON SINCLAIR'S

The Jungle

BY

Eric F. Oatman

SERIES EDITOR

Michael Spring
Editor, *Literary Cavalcade*
Scholastic Inc.

D1526346

BARRON'S EDUCATIONAL SERIES, INC.
Woodbury, New York / London / Toronto / Sydney

ACKNOWLEDGMENTS
We would like to acknowledge the many painstaking hours of work
Holly Hughes and Thomas F. Hirsch have devoted to making the
Book Notes series a success.

All inquiries should be addressed to:
Barron's Educational Series, Inc.
113 Crossways Park Drive
Woodbury, New York 11797

Library of Congress Catalog Card No. 84-18447

International Standard Book No. 0-7641-9114-4

Library of Congress Cataloging in Publication Data
Oatman, Eric F.
    Upton Sinclair's The jungle.

    (Barron's book notes)
    Bibliography: p. 111
    Summary: A guide to reading "The Jungle" with a
critical and appreciative mind. Includes background
on the author's life and times, sample tests, term paper
suggestions, and a reading list.
    1. Sinclair, Upton, 1878–1968. The jungle.
[1. Sinclair, Upton, 1878–1968. The jungle.   2. American
literature—History and criticism]   I. Title
II. Series.
PS3537.I85J976   1984   813'.52   84-18447
ISBN 0-7641-9114-4

PRINTED IN THE UNITED STATES OF AMERICA

456   550   98765432

CONTENTS

ADVISORY BOARD

HOW TO USE THIS BOOK

You have to know how to approach literature in order to get the most out of it. This *Barron's Book Notes* volume follows a plan based on methods used by some of the best students to read a work of literature.

Begin with the guide's section on the author's life and times. As you read, try to form a clear picture of the author's personality, circumstances, and motives for writing the work. This background usually will make it easier for you to hear the author's tone of voice, and follow where the author is heading.

Then go over the rest of the introductory material—such sections as those on the plot, characters, setting, themes, and style of the work. Underline, or write down in your notebook, particular things to watch for, such as contrasts between characters and repeated literary devices. At this point, you may want to develop a system of symbols to use in marking your text as you read. (Of course, you should only mark up a book you own, not one that belongs to another person or a school.) Perhaps you will want to use a different letter for each character's name, a different number for each major theme of the book, a different color for each important symbol or literary device. Be prepared to mark up the pages of your book as you read. Put your marks in the margins so you can find them again easily.

Now comes the moment you've been waiting for—the time to start reading the work of literature. You may want to put aside your *Barron's Book Notes* volume until you've read the work all the way through. Or you may want to alternate, reading the *Book Notes* analysis of each section as soon as you have finished reading the corresponding part of the original. Before you move on, reread crucial passages you don't fully understand. (Don't take this guide's analysis for granted—make up your own mind as to what the work means.)

Once you've finished the whole work of literature, you may want to review it right away, so you can firm up your ideas about what it means. You may want to leaf through the book concentrating on passages you marked in reference to one character or one theme. This is also a good time to reread the *Book Notes* introductory material, which pulls together insights on specific topics.

When it comes time to prepare for a test or to write a paper, you'll already have formed ideas about the work. You'll be able to go back through it, refreshing your memory as to the author's exact words and perspective, so that you can support your opinions with evidence drawn straight from the work. Patterns will emerge, and ideas will fall into place; your essay question or term paper will almost write itself. Give yourself a dry run with one of the sample tests in the guide. These tests present both multiple-choice and essay questions. An accompanying section gives answers to the multiple-choice questions as well as suggestions for writing the essays. If you have to select a term paper topic, you may choose one from the list of suggestions in this book. This guide also provides you with a reading list, to help you when you start research for a term paper, and a selection of provocative comments by critics, to spark your thinking before you write.

THE AUTHOR AND HIS TIMES

Can you remember the pressure that built up inside the last time you had an urge to tell someone off? If you can, you'll understand the fury that prompted Upton Sinclair to write *The Jungle* in 1905.

Sinclair was a cheerful man; yet he loved a fight, especially whenever he felt wronged or saw others being treated unfairly. Instead of responding with physical force to injustice, however, he would reach for his favorite weapon—a pen—and dash off a book, an article, or a play to expose the wrongdoer. Or he'd deliver a speech—or run for public office (in fact, in 1934 he even came close to winning the governorship of California!).

Furious about the amount of control giant industries had over people's lives at the turn of the century in the United States, Sinclair believed that the greed of the men who ran them had turned the American Dream into a nightmare for millions of workers and consumers. And so he wrote *The Jungle* in 1905 to alert the nation to the misery of American workers, and to sketch a solution—socialism—to their problems.

Sinclair's work over the years (including more than eighty books and numerous plays, pamphlets, and speeches) was largely a record of his political passions. With his writings he hoped, literally, to change the world. So, in order to understand *The Jungle*, it's helpful to look at the author's life and at the world he wanted to change in 1905.

Childhood and Youth. Born in Baltimore, Maryland, in 1878, Sinclair grew up there and in New York City as the only child of poor but proud parents. His

mother was the daughter of a well-to-do railroad exec-
utive; his father was the son of a U.S. Navy captain,
who fought and died for the South during the Civil
War. Unfortunately, Upton's father, a liquor sales-
man, drank away most of his earnings, and "home"
to this sad family was a succession of boarding-house
rooms.

Whenever his father failed to pay the rent, a frequent occurrence, Mrs. Sinclair would take Upton to
her father's house or to the home of her wealthy sister. The contrast between his own family's poverty
and his relatives' wealth bewildered him. "Mamma,
why are some children poor and others rich?" he
remembered asking his mother. "How can that be
fair?" As Sinclair noted in his autobiography, those
questions would never stop haunting him:

> Readers of my novels know that I have one favor-
> ite theme, the contrast between the social classes;
> there are characters from both worlds, the rich and
> the poor, and the plots are contrived to carry you
> from one to the other. The explanation is that as far
> back as I can remember, my life was a series of
> Cinderella transformations; one night I would be
> sleeping on a vermin-ridden sofa in a lodging-
> house, and the next night under silken coverlets in
> a fashionable home.

Sinclair's childhood experiences made him a life-
long foe of alcohol, which plays a villain's role in several of his novels, including *The Jungle*. As a teenager
he "traced the saloon to Tammany [the political 'machine' that ran Democratic party politics in New York]
and blamed my troubles on the high chieftains of this
organization. . . . I had not yet found out 'big business.' "

Capitalism.   Big Business was the name given to the
largely unregulated corporations that began to domi-
nate the U.S. economy after the Civil War. The most

harmful ones—those which Sinclair attacked in *The Jungle* and in several other books—were the *trusts*. Trusts were corporations or groups of corporations that were so big, they could monopolize an industry, squeezing out the free competition that can keep prices down. Although a Federal law, the Sherman Anti-Trust Act of 1890, banned such trusts, the government used this weapon sparingly, and some trusts survived well into the 20th century.

The free-booting ways of the trusts were an embarrassment to backers of capitalism, the economic system based on private ownership of the enterprises that produce goods and services. In the 1980s, the U.S. government plays an active role in the nation's capitalist economy. But in the 1800s, the government kept its distance from business. The belief then was that the natural course of supply and demand would regulate the economy to the best interests of everyone.

The trusts made a mockery of that belief by keeping competition down and prices high in the industries they dominated. They did this by gobbling up small companies, some of which might have found a method to produce and sell a product at a lower price.

The trusts trampled on the public interest in other ways, too. Sometimes they corrupted the political process by bribing crooked politicians. During Sinclair's youth, voters who thought elected officials spoke for them were often shocked to find these officials acting solely in the interests of the "Beef Trust," or the "Oil Trust," or some other concentrated industry. As a result, many citizens lost faith in all elected officials.

The trusts had their defenders, however. One of the most well-known was John D. Rockefeller, whose

Standard Oil Company had the petroleum market cornered from 1882 to 1911. "The growth of a large business is merely a survival of the fittest," he said. "The American beauty rose can be produced in the splendor and fragrance which bring cheer to its beholder only by sacrificing the early buds which grow up around it. This is not an evil tendency in business. It is merely the working-out of a law of nature and a law of God."

The courts disagreed and in 1892 ordered the break-up of Rockefeller's trust. It lived on under the guise of a holding company until the courts ordered its dismemberment in 1911.

Socialism.   Sinclair wouldn't turn his attention to the trusts until 1902, when he became acquainted with socialist ideas. *Socialism* is a body of ideas that blames many of society's ills on competition for profit. Socialists want to substitute cooperation for competition. They want the government to control the enterprises that produce goods and services and to direct these enterprises toward socially responsible, not just profitable projects.

As the final chapter of *The Jungle* demonstrates, socialists don't always agree on goals or methods. Some of them want total government control of the economy, some only partial control. Others, including communists, believe that it's necessary to use violence to replace a capitalist system with a socialist one.

Sinclair didn't believe in violent methods or in the need for government to take over an entire economy. From 1902 until his death in 1968, he was a *democratic socialist*. He believed that voters who were educated about the evils of a capitalist system could use the ballot—not the bullet—to take control of the economy through their elected government. The extent of this control would depend on what the voters decided was necessary. Educating the voters was Sinclair's major purpose in writing *The Jungle*.

Early Adulthood.   At age twenty-four, when Sinclair first began reading socialist theory, he was ready for its message. Financially and professionally, he was down and out. He had financed three years of graduate study at Columbia University by churning out cheap adventure novels. Then he had spent two frustrating years writing serious novels, but his serious books had been washouts. He was unable to earn enough money to support his wife and their baby son, and this failure depressed him.

Still, he tried his hand at another novel, *Manassas*, about the Civil War, while living on thirty dollars a month provided by a wealthy socialist. The book was published in 1904 and earned Sinclair five hundred dollars. His total earnings from four novels in four and a half years came to less than a thousand dollars.

Fortunately, Sinclair didn't have to give up writing. The editor of a socialist magazine, the *Appeal to Reason*, offered him $500 for the right to serialize a novel about "wage slaves" (industrial workers). Sinclair snapped up the offer. Leaving his wife and son in Princeton, New Jersey, he took a train to Chicago, which was the world center of the meat-packing industry. He lived among stockyard workers for seven weeks, collecting information for his novel.

What he saw appalled him. There was nothing "enlightened" about the way industrialists of the day viewed their employees. Profits came first; the work-

ers' well-being, second. In the absence of strong
unions, workers were treated brutally and paid wages
much too low for a family to live on.

But the workers dared not complain. Outside the
packing plants, newly arrived immigrants—men and
women desperate for jobs—offered to work for even
lower wages.

Data gathered by the historian Oscar Handlin show
just how desperate they were. For every dollar a
native-born American earned in 1900, Italian immigrants earned 84 cents, Hungarian immigrants 68
cents, and other European immigrants 54 cents.

Sick pay and unemployment benefits, standard in
the 1980s, didn't exist for the average worker in 1904.
When the breadwinner lost his job or was too sick to
work, his family often went hungry.

At the time, there were few laws governing healthy
living and working conditions. The packing plants
were dangerous places—sites of accidents and
sources of all kinds of diseases, from pneumonia and
blood poisoning to deadly tuberculosis. The hovels
where stockyard workers lived were overcrowded
firetraps. The unpaved streets in the slums became
open sewers when rains flooded the cesspools behind
the houses.

Sinclair also noted how little the government did to
protect consumers against fraud. Sawdust and rat
droppings were mixed into the sausage meat and dev-
iled ham. Spoiled meat regularly found its way into
cans. One U.S. Army general estimated that spoiled
meat, first treated with dangerous chemicals and then
canned, had killed three thousand U.S. soldiers during the Spanish-American War in 1898.

To survive, workers in the meat-packing plants
were forced to take part in this horrendous fraud—
one that affected nearly every American. Moreover,

the poor and uneducated workers were frequently swindled into buying furniture, houses, insurance, and other things they couldn't afford, usually signing contracts they couldn't understand.

Sinclair's Research. Sinclair was a good reporter. He checked and double-checked his facts. He talked with settlement house workers—men and women who had opted to live among Chicago's poor immigrants and help them "settle" in America.

Once he had the facts, he had to dream up people to "hang" them on. He tells in his autobiography how he put together his story:

> Wandering about "back of the yards" one Sunday afternoon I saw a wedding party going into the rear room of a saloon. . . . [Sunday was the only day the workers had free.] I slipped into the room and stood against the wall. There, the opening chapter of *The Jungle* began to take form. There were my characters—the bride, the groom, the old mother and father, the boisterous cousin, the children, the three musicians, everybody. I . . . began to write the scene in my mind, going over it and, as was my custom, fixing it fast. I . . . stayed until late at night, . . . not talking to anyone, just watching, imagining, and engraving the details on my mind. It was two months before I . . . first put pen to paper; but the story stayed, and I wrote down whole paragraphs, whole pages, exactly as I had memorized them.

Back in Princeton, the Sinclairs borrowed some money and moved out of their one-room cabin into a farmhouse. Behind the house, Sinclair set up a rickety cabin, 8 feet wide and 10 feet long. He equipped it with a potbelly stove, a chair, and a table, and began writing *The Jungle* on Christmas Day, 1904.

His experiences in Chicago had shocked him. Nonetheless, the book's emotional energy, from the first page to the last, comes primarily from Sinclair and his family's own suffering.

The *Appeal to Reason* began serializing *The Jungle* even before it was finished. The weekly, published in Kansas, had about 500,000 subscribers, mostly farmers in the Midwest and West. Readers began to write to Sinclair, and he saw he had a success on his hands.

Nonetheless, a number of book publishers refused to handle *The Jungle*. One wanted Sinclair to cut out some of the graphic descriptions of packing-plant operations. Others, no doubt, wanted nothing to do with a book that aimed to convert the nation to socialism. Finally, one publisher sent a lawyer to Chicago to check out Sinclair's facts. The lawyer's report backed Sinclair, and the firm brought out the book in January 1906.

Muckrakers.   *The Jungle* caused a furor. The book's revelations became front-page news. Sinclair's shocking picture of packing-plant conditions made a nation of meat-eaters groan with pain and anger. President Theodore Roosevelt sent a commission to Chicago to investigate the charges of this new "muckraker."

Muckraker was Roosevelt's word for writers like Sinclair, who exposed business abuses and political corruption. Roosevelt read their work and even consulted with them. (It was at a White House lunch with Sinclair that Roosevelt decided to send his own investigators to Chicago.) But he claimed not to care much for them, possibly because they attacked many of the politicians and business leaders he had to work with as president.

Historians point out that muckrakers served a useful purpose. Most of them wrote for large-circulation magazines that had the money to support thorough investigations. Their reports helped drum up public support for government regulation of the trusts and for electoral reforms that made politics in the U.S. more democratic.

Sinclair's muckraking in *The Jungle* helped clean up the meat-packing industry. Roosevelt's commission upheld all of Sinclair's charges, except one about men falling into vats and being turned into lard. (Sinclair's informants in Chicago insisted this had happened— not once, but several times.) As a result, the president put the power of his office behind two bills designed to reform the industry.

The Pure Food and Drug Act banned the selling of dangerous or fake drugs and impure food. The Meat Inspection Act required federal officials to inspect meat slaughtered in one state and sold in another. Both became law in June 1906, less than six months after *The Jungle* appeared in book form.

Sinclair's work had had a major effect—but not the one he had hoped it would. He felt that the uproar over spoiled and adulterated meat had caused his readers to miss his larger message, and he spelled out his disappointment in a magazine article that appeared in October 1906:

> I wished to frighten the country by a picture of what its industrial masters were doing to their victims; entirely by chance I had stumbled on another discovery—what they were doing to the meat-supply of the civilized world. In other words, I aimed at the public's heart, and by accident I hit it in the stomach.

The message of *The Jungle* was not lost on fellow socialists, however. Jack London, a prominent socialist and best-selling author, touted the novel in the pages of the *Age of Reason*:

> Here it is at last! The book we have been waiting for these many years! The *Uncle Tom's Cabin* of wage slavery! Comrade Sinclair's book, *The Jungle*! And what *Uncle Tom's Cabin* did for black slaves, *The Jungle* has a large chance to do for the wage-slaves of today.

Uncle Tom's Cabin, Harriet Beecher Stowe's 1852 novel, troubled the nation's conscience with a painful portrait of the evils of slavery. It was one of the many wedges that drove Northerners and Southerners apart and brought on the war that put an end to slavery in America.

The Jungle failed to arouse a similar response for the "working men of America," to whom it is dedicated. Most Americans in 1906 seemed to accept Rockefeller's claim that the worker's sacrifice was part of God's design. Government programs designed to protect workers on the job and during periods of unemployment wouldn't arrive until the bleak days of the Great Depression in the 1930s.

Yet the novel's failure to extend democracy to the workplace is no reflection on Sinclair's abilities as a reporter. *The Jungle* is a heartbreaking story of an immigrant family's struggle to survive, and for that alone it is well worth reading. But it is also a sound historical document of the life and sufferings of factory workers during the early years of this century.

THE NOVEL

The Plot

The wedding feast of Jurgis Rudkis and Ona Lukos-zaite, immigrants from Lithuania, begins exuberantly and ends in disappointment in the back room of a Chicago saloon. Most of the guests are drunk and exhausted. The thought of having to return to work in the stockyards in a few short hours further depresses them.

For the newlyweds' relatives—especially Marija Berczynskas, Ona's cousin and the organizer of the festivities—there is further reason for despair. In the old country, the guests chipped in to pay for the wedding party and to leave the newlyweds a little extra money with which to start their married life. Yet here in Packington, the stockyard district of Chicago, the old communal traditions are dying out among the immigrant workers. So many freeloaders have come to the party that Jurgis and Ona must begin their married life in debt.

Still, Jurgis faces the future bravely. "Leave it to me," he tells Ona. "I will earn more money—I will work harder."

Jurgis first saw Ona a year and a half earlier, at a fair in Lithuania, where he had gone to sell two of his father's horses. She was fourteen, and he was about twenty five. It was love at first sight for Jurgis, but Ona's father, "a rich man," would not let Jurgis have her. The next time he saw her, her father had died, the farm had been sold, and the family was adrift. Still, Ona's attachment to her stepmother, Elzbieta, kept her from marrying Jurgis.

Jonas, Elizbieta's brother, suggested that they might have a better future in America, where a friend had become rich in a city named Chicago. They set out—six adults (including Jurgis's father, Dede Antanas) and Elizbieta's six children—in early summer.

Once in Chicago, the first order of business was to find shelter and work. Jonas's friend, Kokubas Szedvilas, a poor delicatessen owner, acted as their guide. He sent them to a filthy lodging house, where they determined to stay only until they got work.

Jurgis found work as a sweeper on the killing beds at Brown's, a meat-packing company. Marija found work as a can painter, and Jonas got a job pushing a truck at Durham's, Brown's rival. Though at first Dede Antanas couldn't find work, they decided they could afford to buy a "new" house, using some of their savings as a down payment. Finally, Dede Antanas got a job in the damp "pickle room" at Durham's by promising to kick back a third of his salary to the man who hired him.

That experience and others began to shake Jurgis's faith in America. Both Jonas and Marija had gotten their jobs through the misfortunes of others. In his job Antanas had to shovel the residue of chemically treated meat onto a truck headed for the cannery. Jurgis saw pregnant cows butchered and their unborn calves illegally mixed with other carcasses. He even helped butcher cattle that had died before reaching the slaughterhouse.

His faith was further shaken when he heard their house was not in fact new. The previous four families had lost the house when they couldn't keep up monthly payments. Jurgis also finds out there were hidden charges to be paid each month—for interest, taxes, and so on.

Ona got a job sewing covers on hams, and 14-year-old Stanislovas convinced a priest to certify he was sixteen—old enough to hold a job. Stanislovas then joined the army of child workers by getting a job at Durham's placing empty cans under jets of lard, 10 hours a day, six days a week, for five cents an hour. Working this way, the family was able to save enough money for the November wedding of Ona and Jurgis.

All are back at work the morning after the wedding—mostly dead on their feet from exhaustion. Jurgis and Ona's married life is cheerless. The pressures of work, poverty, and illness stifle their spirits. Jurgis's father, Antanas, sickens and dies, and Jurgis, learning fast, negotiates a funeral that won't bankrupt the family.

Winter comes, an agony for Packingtown. Homeless men who had spent the warmer months in the country, working on farms, clamor at the gates of the packing houses, looking for work. Inside the plants, there is no heat, except in the cooking rooms. At lunch break, the men race to "Whiskey Row," where, for the price of a drink or two, they can keep warm and get a "free" lunch. Jurgis takes only one drink, for he has Ona to think about. The house is cold, and many nights they sleep with their clothes on.

Marija and Tamoszius Kuszleika fall in love, but the canning factory where Marija works shuts down, and they must postpone their wedding. A general business slowdown means that Jurgis gets only about a half day's paid work, though he must spend all day on the killing floor.

Angry, Jurgis joins the union and has the other working members of his family join as well. He begins to learn English. He also acquires a cynical opinion of democracy. A Democratic party member helps him become a citizen and vote for the candidates of the local Democratic boss, Mike Scully. In exchange for his vote, Jurgis gets two dollars and two hours off work, with pay.

He begins to see how the packers operate. They sell spoiled or adulterated meat without qualms. Their workers are exposed to awful occupational diseases, yet the packers take no steps to protect the employees. They steal water from the city and pollute the Chicago River—and the city government looks the other way.

Jurgis's family struggles through their second winter in America. Spring comes, with its flooding rains, and then summer, with its stifling heat. Marija's factory reopens, but she loses her job anyway and becomes a meat trimmer at half her first wage. Ona has a baby boy and harms her health by returning to work prematurely.

Their third winter, Jurgis injures himself on the job and is out of work for three months. When spring arrives, Jonas simply disappears, reducing the family's income by a third. Two of Elzbieta's boys leave school to sell newspapers. When Jurgis feels fit to work, he finds his old job gone. Finally, he takes a job at Durham's fertilizer plant. Elzbieta goes to work, and the boys go to school again. Jurgis, a pariah because of the smell of fertilizer he carries with him, starts to drink. Ona is pregnant again and prey to fits of weeping. Jurgis discovers that she has been sleeping with Phil Connor, one of the bosses, who threatened to have everyone in her family fired if she didn't submit to him. Jurgis nearly kills Connor and is sent to jail. Stanislovas visits him and reports that Ona is sick, Marija injured, and the family almost starving. Their only income is from what the children can earn selling newspapers.

After his release from jail, Jurgis discovers that the family has been evicted from the house they had struggled so hard to keep. They are back in the lodging house where they first lived when they came to the city. Jurgis finds Ona in labor and persuades a midwife to help, to no avail. Ona and the baby die.

Because of his little son Antanas, Jurgis stays and gets a job with a maker of farm equipment. After nine days, his department closes, and Jurgis is laid off. He gets another job at a steel plant. When his son accidentally drowns, Jurgis turns his back on Chicago and becomes a hobo. In the fall he returns to the city and gets a job digging a tunnel. An on-the-job injury puts him in the hospital. After he gets out, he joins the army of unemployed men hunting for work during a recession in January 1904.

He starts begging and meets the drunken scion of a meat-packing family. Jurgis goes home with him and leaves with a full stomach and a hundred-dollar bill. When a bartender cheats him out of the money Jurgis attacks him, is arrested and jailed.

Released again, he returns to crime, tutored by a former cellmate named Jack Duane. Jurgis learns how Chicago's criminal underworld helps to corrupt the city's government. Through Buck Halloran, a district leader, he learns how graft works, and he learns about "pull."

Jurgis returns to the stockyards as an undercover operative of the Democratic boss. He promotes the boss's choice for alderman—the Republican candidate. Jurgis's man wins, and Jurgis stays on in the stockyards. In June, the butcher's union strikes. Jurgis gets a foreman's job, takes bribes from his men, and beats up strikers for the packers. A second attack on Phil Connor lands him in jail again. Jurgis posts bail and flees.

He goes back to begging. He meets an old friend who gives him Marija's address. When he tracks her down, he discovers she is a prostitute and a drug addict. Stanislovas is dead, she explains—eaten by rats. The others are alive, living mainly on Marija's earnings.

That night he walks into a political rally to keep warm. An emotional orator converts him to socialism, and his life takes a new turn. He is given a job as porter in a hotel owned by a socialist. He lives with Elzbieta and her children, but cannot convince Marija to change her life. Jurgis throws himself into social-ism. The novel ends on election night in 1904. At a Socialist party gathering, Jurgis learns that his party has made a strong showing. A speaker exhorts the crowd to organize the workers so that "Chicago will be ours!"

The Characters

Sinclair populates *The Jungle* with characters from nearly every walk of life and social class. He gives 60 of them names. Dozens of others go nameless, although their actions help shape the destinies of the major characters. Together, the men, women, and children in *The Jungle* suggest the vibrant and varied life of America during the early years of the 20th cen-tury.

The suggestion is intentional on Sinclair's part, since his goal is to expose an entire social system—the ruthlessly competitive capitalist democracy that is the chief villain of his story. He seeks to prove that all who come into contact with the system are brutalized and corrupted by it.

A brief analysis of some of the important characters follows. The characters are listed in the order of their appearance.

Marija Berczynskas

Marija, Ona's cousin, is one of the most striking characters in the novel. She is the one we'd bet on if asked to predict which member of the family had the best chance of surviving. When we meet her on the first page, she is in charge of the wedding feast, seeing that "the best home traditions" are respected. Later we learn that she has a "face full of boundless good nature and the muscles of a dray horse"—characteristics that helped her get her first job in America, painting cans.

Yet she has a softness about her, as well. Tamoszius discovers this and falls in love with her.

By the end of the novel, however, she is a whore and dope addict, burned-out at the age of 24 or 25. Her remarkable health has disappeared with the Old World values that served her so poorly. She now takes "the business point of view"; prostitution is simply a way of making a living in the new world—of surviving. "When people are starving," she says, "and they have anything with a price, they ought to sell it, I say."

What has happened to bring down this female counterpart of Jurgis? She has had a lot of discouragement: job injuries, layoffs, her family's dissolution.

The final blow must have been Tamoszius's disappearance after he lost a finger and could no longer play the violin. We see her in the final chapter, having given herself up to her fate. "I'll stay here till I die, I guess. It's all I'm fit for."

Ona Lukoszaite

Ona is her husband's opposite, and Sinclair introduces her as such. She is "blue-eyed and fair, while Jurgis had great black eyes with beetling brows." She has some education: he has none. She is tiny "small for her age, a mere child"; Jurgis is huge, with "mighty shoulders" and "giant hands." Clearly, she's going to need protection in the predatory environment of Chicago. The question from the start is whether Jurgis can provide it. In the end, he cannot. She dies in childbirth at the age of 18, four years after they'd met and two years after they'd married, having lived less than three years in America.

The years between are brutal and take their toll on her body and mind. Too timid to assert herself, she is cheated out of a trolley transfer and must walk through rain to her job sewing covers on hams. After childbirth, she returns to work too early and suffers "womb trouble." Her coughing suggests she may have tuberculosis. She suffers "fearful nervousness" and "fits of aimless weeping"—all attributable, we later learn, to her secret life as mistress of a boss who is forcing her to submit to him. "He would have ruined us," she told Jurgis. "I only did it—to save us."

Was hers a heroic act, as some readers suggest? Or is she simply a passive victim—an easy prey for all the forces arrayed against immigrant workers in industrial America? The correct answer probably lies some where in between. Unable to afford proper medical help, she dies in agony trying to bear a stillborn child.

Jurgis Rudkus

A young Lithuanian immigrant, Jurgis is the book's central character. He is a naïf—a familiar figure in literature—who gains wisdom after a series of batterings push him into the pit of despair. His discovery of socialism points the way out, and at the end of the novel he becomes a convert, happily immersed in a movement that promises to bring economic democracy to America.

Jurgis is the only character whose interior life is explored. Yet Sinclair's handling of his emotions, moods, and thoughts doesn't add much to our knowledge of him. Like the other characters, he is revealed most vividly through his actions and losses.

Jurgis's primary goal is to protect Ona, and when he reaches America, he has every confidence he can do so. He is strong, young, and eager to work, and a true believer in "rugged individualism"—self-reliance. But the forces of greed overpower him. A real estate agent cons the family into buying a house they can't afford. Then after a job injury lays him up for three months, he loses his job and must accept one in a fertilizer plant. In the end, he can't protect Ona. She is forced into prostitution and dies trying to give birth to a second child. Economic forces, due to a slack in demand, cost him a job at a farm equipment plant. After his son drowns, he quits another job at a steel plant and spends a summer on the road, experimenting with freedom from responsibility. Back in Chicago, he gets a job digging a tunnel. An injury lands him in the hospital.

After these events, he sinks into a life of crime as a
foe of society. He becomes a mugger and a grafter. He
dupes fellow workers as an undercover operative for
the Democratic machine. He helps break up a strike
then ends up in jail a third time. Once more he
becomes a homeless man, a beggar. So much for rugged individualism!

It is by chance that he is saved. He walks into a
Socialist rally for warmth and becomes swept up in
the movement. Here, at last, is an explanation for his
woes and a road map to utopia. Socialism revives his
dignity, strength, and self-confidence because he is
now a member of something larger than himself, no
merely an individual. In the last scene, he vanishes
into an audience of two thousand Socialists who are
attending an election-night rally.

Teta Elzbieta Lukoszaite

Ona's beloved stepmother, and herself the mother
of six children, Elzbieta remains a link between the
Old World and the New throughout the novel. She
insists on a traditional wedding for Ona and a proper
funeral for her son Kristoforas, when he dies. She
begs money for a requiem mass when Ona dies and
persuades Jurgis to stay on for his son's sake. She is
ready, predictable, even stoic. She is "one of the prim
itive creatures: like the angleworm, which goes on liv
ing though cut in half. . . . She did this because it was
her nature—she asked no questions about the justice
of it, nor the worthwhileness of life in which destruc
tion and death ran riot."

Although we know all these things *about* her, we
don't really get to know her. At the end, though sick
and being supported largely by Marija's prostitution
she attends Socialist meetings with Jurgis; yet the

mean nothing to her—she plans her meals during the speeches.

Kotrina Lukoszaite

Kotrina, Elzbieta's daughter, suffers the fate of many working-class females when she has to shoulder the burden of keeping house at age 13. She is "prematurely made old," Sinclair tells us. Like her brothers, she eventually goes out to sell newspapers and becomes the most successful of them all.

Grandmother Majauskiene

This wise old woman, the first Socialist we meet, seems to enjoy being the bearer of bad news. It is she who tells the family that the real estate agent swindled them. Sinclair describes her as a witch—"unrelenting, typifying fate." Like Shakespeare's witches, she foreshadows the future. The family's house, she says, is "unlucky."

Tamoszius Kusleika

Tamoszius is a slaughterhouse worker and also a self-taught musician, whose energy inspires the gaiety of the wedding feast, despite his lack of talent. His love for Marija (his opposite in size and manner) is doomed; the two can never get enough money together to marry. After he loses a finger on the job and can no longer play the violin, he disappears. He is a comic figure and, ultimately, a tragic one. A Socialist, he is proof that the creed is not every convert's salvation.

Dede Antanas Rudkus

Jurgis's father is a touching figure, who thinks he is dying when we first meet him at the wedding feast. He is sixty years old but looks eighty. His gloomy speech, delivered amid consumptive coughs, throws the mood of the feast off-kilter.

While working in the pickle (chemical) room at Durham's, the old man contracts tuberculosis and sores that never heal on his feet. But, a proud man, he continues working almost until his death.

Jokubas Szedvilas

Jokubas is the friend of Jonas whose mythical success in America lures the families of Jurgis and Ona to Chicago. Actually, he is a delicatessen owner who has had to mortgage his store to pay back rent. He finds the newcomers a place to stay and takes them on a tour of the packing plants. His sarcastic comments annoy Jurgis, as does his advice *not* to buy a house. In both cases, he is proven right.

Aniele Jukneiene

A "little woman, with a wrinkled face," Aniele is the rheumatic widow whose "unthinkably filthy" lodging house becomes the newcomers' first home in Chicago. She supports her three children by raising chickens and taking in wash and lodgers. After Ona and her family are evicted from their house, she rents her garret to them. There, Ona dies and, later, little Antanas drowns outside the house.

Jonas

Elzbieta's brother is the one who suggests the family emigrate to America, where "a friend of his had gotten rich." In Chicago, he gets work pushing a hand truck and likes "to smoke his pipe in peace before . . . bed." One Saturday night he picks up his pay and disappears. Though the family's income is reduced by a third, no one blames him. "He paid good board, and was yet obliged to live in a family where nobody had enough to eat."

Stanislovas Lukoszaite

Stanislovas, one of Elzbieta's children, is the center of Sinclair's exposé of child labor; he goes to work at a lard machine at age fourteen. His shock at seeing a young worker lose his ears from frostbite gives him a pathological fear of cold. To get him to work on cold days, Jurgis must beat him. Eventually, Stanislovas loses his job and goes into the streets to sell newspapers. He falls asleep in an old oil factory after drinking too much beer, and rats eat him alive.

Bush Harper

Harper, one of Scully's henchmen, is the night watchman who helps Jurgis become naturalized, so that he can vote the Democratic ticket. Later he gets Jurgis a job at Durham's as an undercover political worker for Mike Scully, the Democratic boss.

Mike Scully

Scully is the corrupt political boss of the stockyards district. A puppet of the packers, he nevertheless has a lot of power. Through a number of crooked schemes, he obtains enough money to bribe officials and pay for votes.

Miss Henderson

Ona gets her job sewing covers on hams by paying a bribe to her forelady, Miss Henderson. Henderson lives in a brothel with Phil Connor. She sets up Ona for Connor's sexual pleasure.

Little Antanas Rudkus

Jurgis's child makes a family man out of Jurgis, and it's for his sake that Jurgis goes to work after Ona dies. His drowning in the flooded street outside the widow's lodging house drives Jurgis away to follow his whims for the summer.

Vilimas and Nikalojus Lukoszaite

Two of Elzbieta's sons, Vilimas, age 11, and Nikalojus, age 10, are pulled out of school and sent into the streets to sell newspapers. They become streetwise, adapting too well to their new environment to suit their elders, learning to sneak free rides on trolleys and to identify the city's criminals by name.

Kristoforas Lukoszaite

At the age of three, Elzbieta's crippled child Kristoforas dies of convulsions, possibly from eating spoiled sausage. His loss devastates his mother, who begs the money for a proper funeral.

Pat Callahan

The owner of saloons and brothels, this city judge does the packers' bidding whenever he's asked. He ignores Jurgis's honest defense of his attack on Connor and sentences Jurgis to jail.

Madame Haupt

One of Sinclair's most convincing characters, this midwife is a grotesque—a repugnant clown figure that invites the reader's nervous laughter. Fat, greasy, vain, and greedy, she nonetheless goes to Ona's aid because she can't stand to see people suffer. Sinclair uses her to make a point about medical care for the poor.

Juozapas Lukoszaite

Another of Elzbieta's crippled children, Juozapas pokes his crutch into the garbage dump looking for edible food. A social worker discovers him and sets up a job for Jurgis at a steel plant.

Freddie Jones

Son of the wealthy meat packer, Old Man Jones, young Freddie is out on the town when he finds Jurgis begging. Sinclair uses him to show the insensitivity of the rich to the plight of the poor. Freddie can't make the imaginative leap required to understand Jurgis's poverty. He figures they're both in the same boat: "No money, either," Freddie tells Jurgis. His father has left him "with less than two thousand dollars in his pocket," more than an unskilled worker in Packingtown can make in five years.

Buck Halloran

One of Scully's men, Halloran introduces Jurgis to some of the intricacies of political corruption. He pays Jurgis $5 to pick up paychecks for imaginary city workers. He's another example of the people who bleed city governments and corrupt the political process.

Comrade Ostrinski

A Polish immigrant, this struggling pants-finisher lives with his wife in a dingy flat. He takes Jurgis home and give him a crash course in Socialist theory.

Tommy Hinds

Hinds, a veteran of the Civil War and a Socialist, hires Jurgis to be the porter in his hotel—a "hot-bed of . . . propaganda." There, Jurgis continues his Socialist education. Whatever the complaint, Hinds has the cure: "Vote the Socialist ticket!"

Other Elements

SETTING

Most of the action in *The Jungle* takes place from November 1900 to November 1904 in Chicago, Illinois, then "the meat capital of the world." In flashbacks (chapters 2 through 6) Sinclair takes the reader back to the spring of 1899 and rural Lithuania, then part of Tsarist Russia. (Today Lithuania is one of the republics that make up the Soviet Union.) This device allows Sinclair to fill in background details about Jurgis, Ona, and their families. More important, it allows him to contrast peasant life in the Old World with the jarring brutality of life for industrial workers in America.

But Chicago is the main setting—and a brilliant choice it was. As the 20th century opened, Chicago produced more factory goods than any other city in the world except New York. Best of all, for Sinclair's purposes, it had the meat-packing industry, a ready-made metaphor for everything that Sinclair believed ugly and life-denying about a capitalist economy.

About 8.8 million immigrants entered the U.S. between 1901 and 1910. Most were lured to the big cities, where—if they were lucky—they got backbreaking jobs as unskilled laborers in factories and mills. To Sinclair, their fate was no different from that of the hogs and cattle brought to Chicago by train from all over the Midwest and West. The immigrants were being led to slaughter, too. Work in the meat-packing industry was notoriously hazardous.

THEMES

In 1905 Sinclair had two goals in writing *The Jungle*. He wanted to expose the evils of capitalism—especially the way it exploited wage earners. And he wanted to convince his readers to consider socialism as an alternative to capitalism. Thus, the novel has two major themes:

1. Greed and ruthless competition have made turn-of-the-century America into a brutal jungle. "Take or be taken" is the guiding rule, and everyone is someone else's prey. "All the fair and noble impulses of humanity, the dreams of poets and the agonies of martyrs, are shackled and bound in the service of organized and predatory Greed."

2. The solution is to substitute cooperation for competition by reorganizing the economy along So- cialist lines—that is, by giving ownership of essential industries to the public and running them democrati- cally for everyone's benefit.

Linked to these major themes are a number of minor themes:

1. Those at the bottom of the economic ladder— wage-earners and their families—are at a particular disadvantage in the capitalist jungle. They are slaves to the whims of their masters—the capitalists who own and run private industry. Immigrants, ignorant of the language and ways of their new country, are the most vulnerable members of this class.

2. Industrial capitalism is an efficient, impersonal "slaughtering machine" that sacrifices its workers. Businesses take no responsibility for their workers. They "use up" the strong and young and discard the weak and old.

3. Democracy under capitalism is a sham, because big business, not the ordinary citizen, controls the government. Business and government work hand-

in-hand to corrupt the democratic process. Elective politics is a shell game that the worker usually loses.

4.   Unions are no match for capitalist organizations, whose superior resources make them quicker, stronger, and more flexible. "The whole machinery of society is at their aggressors' command."

5.   Because they are often ignorant of their own best interests, workers unknowingly take steps to defeat them. They back the wrong candidates, manufacture goods that might harm them, and break strikes that could benefit them.

6.   Wage earners must be taught to see themselves for what they are: an oppressed class. Only then can they be expected to act in their own interests and to elect leaders who will support a Socialist revolution.

7.   Marriage is a trap, because the need to support a family makes wage-earners vulnerable to exploitation, on the job and off.

8.   The consumer's welfare, like the worker's, is of secondary importance to the capitalist, who puts profits first.

Many readers have remarked on Sinclair's kinship with the Naturalist school of literature founded by the noted French author Émile Zola (1840–1902). Sinclair's characters, for example, are creatures of circumstance—of the accidents of their pasts (through heredity and culture) and their present environments. It is useful in a discussion of the novel's themes to examine the Naturalists' theories. As you read *The Jungle,* you can decide how close a kin Zola is to Sinclair.

Zola developed Naturalism as a way of justifying the realist approach in literature. Realists describe things as they are, without dressing up what they find important in everyday life.

Zola believed that, in literature, realism was the only honest approach. He also believed that in the hands of a careful realist the novel could be a kind of scientific experiment. So notebook in hand, Zola studied the world of his characters—usually Parisian slum dwellers. He recorded the details of that world in his novels to show how his characters' environments shaped their lives. Moreover, he was careful to trace each of his characters' ancestries in order to show that a person's fate was as much the result of heredity as of environment. Thus, Zola's novels were, in effect, laboratory tests on imaginary people.

Many readers of *The Jungle* argue that Sinclair adopted Zola's technique and used it to prove his case against capitalism. Other readers feel it is misleading to call Sinclair a Zolaist. For one thing, Zola believed that one's nature—whether good or evil, for instance—was completely determined by heredity. Sinclair didn't share this belief. In *The Jungle* he puts the blame for the wrongs people commit against one another on the environment. It's the economic system, he says, that forces people to be evil in order to survive.

As might be expected, Sinclair's cure for weaknesses in human nature also differed from Zola's. Zola believed that a combination of medicine and education could overcome the effects of heredity and lead to the perfection of human nature. Sinclair's cure for the ills of industrial America was a new environment—a socialist economy, where cooperation would replace competition.

There are other differences between the two writers' approaches to their subjects. Zola's characters are trapped in a web of circumstance from which they cannot escape. His books end tragically, without hope. *The Jungle*, however, ends on a positive note— with a socialist victory in sight, if not in hand. And Jurgis is not trapped. On the contrary, his discovery of socialism and conversion to it liberates him.

Finally, there's nothing dispassionately scientific about Sinclair's approach to his subject. You know whose side he's on as soon as you read the book's dedication: "To the Workingmen of America." *The Jungle* is not a cool-headed clinical experiment of the sort Zola felt he was conducting. It's an unvarnished piece of propaganda for socialism and against the destructive form of capitalism that was practiced in Sinclair's day.

STYLE

Sinclair's style is simple and direct. He was not a "literary" writer, interested in using language in new or startling ways to advance the form of the novel. "Few writers seemed to write less for the sake of literature," the critic Alfred Kazin has written of Sinclair's work as a whole. "First things came first; the follies of capitalism, the dangers of drinking, the iniquities of wealthy newspapers and universities came first."

Still, in *The Jungle* Sinclair uses language effectively, and in a variety of ways, to shape his characters and develop his themes. Direct statement is his strength, but he makes good use of symbols, too. A description of a hog slaughtering turns out to be an allegory about the immigrant's fate in industrial America. (See the

discussion of chapter 3.) Belching smokestacks and
the smell of rotting garbage suggests an impression of
hell on earth. (See chapter 2.)

Sinclair uses strong sensory imagery that many of
his more refined readers in 1906 found repugnant.
Stockyards and dumps are smelly places—Sinclair
makes sure we know just how smelly. He makes us
hear the "broom, broom" of a cello and feel the slippery flesh that makes work so dangerous for beef
boners. He makes us see what, in ordinary life, we
might recoil from: garbage, the slaughtering process,
a greasy midwife with blood "splashed upon her
clothing and her face."

Sinclair relies heavily on figures of speech (metaphors and similes) to remind us that he's serious
about comparing life in turn-of-the-century America
with life in a jungle. Enraged, Jurgis breathes deeply
"like a wounded bull" (simile). His foe, Connor, is
"the great beast" (metaphor).

Like the symbolism, such figures of speech help
give many passages in the book a poetic quality, forcing you to dig beneath the surface of the words for
meaning.

But you never have to dig too deeply. There's nothing deceptive about Sinclair. He wants you to understand him easily and well.

POINT OF VIEW

Who's telling the story? Whose point of view does
the narrator reflect?

The answer depends on which narrator you're talking about, for there are at least two narrators in *The
Jungle*. One, the omniscient author, is rather god-like
and all-knowing, setting scenes, summarizing events,

and moving in and out of different characters' minds. The other is more of a commentator—an editorial writer who lashes out at one iniquity or another, telling us what to look at and how to think about what we see. This second narrator often knows more than his characters do, and he's not shy about sharing his insights with us.

The narrator's double identity can be confusing. At one point, the omniscient narrator describes some police officers and some strike-breaking goons, including Jurgis, taking off after strikers. In the fracas, Jurgis and a couple of cops break up and rob a saloon. The second narrator tells us what Jurgis cannot possibly know—that a few thousand biased newspapers will report the episode as a riot, a reason to condemn the strikers. Sinclair obviously thought he needed the switch in narrators to make his statement.

He makes similar switches elsewhere, especially in muckraking passages. Sinclair is an incurable explainer. When he thinks that the conventional narrator can't get his point across, he steps in himself. But not once do we view a scene through the eyes of one of his characters.

FORM AND STRUCTURE

The Jungle consists of 31 chapters, all designed to move the reader—and its hero—along the path to socialism. On the way, our guide (Sinclair) makes us pause and examine the surrounding landscape—the jungle of predators, the prey and the traps for the weak or unwary. It's here—in the form of short or long passages—that the muckraking takes place, exposing the absurdities of the economic system or the perfidies of the packers and crooked public officials. As might be expected, the pacing of the plot is somewhat jerky. Sinclair rushes to tell his story, then stops in his tracks—for a paragraph or a whole section of a chapter—to explore a subject that outrages him.

Overall, the novel follows a conversion pattern—one in which its hero passes through stages of pride, doubt, and despair, to his awakening and salvation. Jurgis is, for the most part, in the grip of forces beyond his control, though eventually he finds his footing and takes control of his life.

The Story

The word propaganda has a negative ring to it today. We usually use it to mean a systematic effort—in the press or through art, for example—to spread ideas that are probably false. Furthermore, we tend to think that propaganda has no place in novels or paintings.

Sinclair rejected the word's negative connotation and the bias against propaganda in art. To him, propaganda was simply an attempt to convince others of one's point of view. And far from diluting art, propaganda strengthened it, Sinclair felt.

In the chapter-by-chapter analysis that follows, we will look at The Jungle primarily as Sinclair did—as a propaganda novel and a call to arms. We will examine the techniques he used to sell his particular vision of industrial capitalism and his prescription for a cure.

Some of the techniques he uses are found more often in nonfiction than in fiction. Sinclair leans heavily upon the documentary approach of the historian, for example. At times, he approaches his subject as if he were a muckraker composing an exposé for a magazine. At other times—particularly in the final chapters—he makes a direct, reasoned appeal to the reader, much like a pamphlet writer.

Clearly, Sinclair wears several hats in *The Jungle*. He is a dramatizer, a historian, a muckraker, and a pamphleteer. (Some readers argue that he wears a fifth hat—that of a Naturalist disciple of the French novelist, Émile Zola. See the Themes section of this guide.) For a full appreciation of *The Jungle*, it will be helpful if you learn to sort out the different roles the author plays.

CHAPTER 1

Sinclair uses the opening chapter to introduce you to his major characters and their Old World values, and to foreshadow the tragic events to come. This chapter demonstrates how gifted he is as a dramatizer.

The book opens in medias res—Latin for in the middle of things. It's four o'clock on a Sunday afternoon in November 1900. The wedding of Ona Lukoszaite and Jurgis Rudkus is over, and the wedding feast is about to begin. The guests are arriving at a saloon, whose back room has been rented for the occasion.

Without doubt, this is an event—not just for the wedding party, but for the children who live back of the yards in Chicago's stockyard district, which Sinclair calls Packingtown. Marija Berczynskas, Ona's cousin and the impatient organizer of the day, has been accusing her carriage driver of dawdling "all the way down Ashland Avenue." Her exuberance has attracted a crowd of adults and children, some of whom will be invited to join the *veselija*, as the wedding feast is called.

NOTE: Use of Contrasts Keep an eye throughout the chapter on the way Sinclair uses contrasts to create characters. "Ona was blue-eyed and fair, while Jurgis had great black eyes with beetling brows." Jurgis has "mighty shoulders and . . . giant hands," yet, as the party begins, he is timid to the point of seeming as "frightened as a hunted animal."

The party—like any party—opens with great expectations among the guests. And, for the most part, their expectations are fulfilled. It is a joyful occasion, especially in its opening hours. But there's an unmistakable undercurrent of sadness here, of pain. Before the party ends, that sadness will become the dominant mood. By then, most everyone will be drunk or asleep or both, but Teta Elzbieta, Ona's stepmother, and Marija, usually unconquerable, will be "sobbing loudly."

Why? What has caused this Old World custom of the *veselija*—one to which the poor Lithuanians in Packingtown "cling with all the power of their souls—to turn sour? Sinclair drops a lot of clues throughout this earthy, bittersweet chapter. In so doing, he hints at many of the tragedies that lie ahead. The chapter's mood swings—from optimism to despair and back to a guarded optimism—foreshadow the novel's pattern and the emotional rollercoaster ride that Jurgis is about to embark on.

As we learn, the guests are happiest when they can forget not only their cares, but where they are and what they are—peasants transplanted to an alien, unforgiving environment. And, for a while, they are able to do this. In a tiny room, they try to recreate, just for a day, the traditions of the Old World. Led by

Marija, the women bustle about, cooking and serving food. The musicians, led by Tamoszius Kuszeleika, play badly, but no one cares. "This music is their music, music of home. It stretches out its arms to them. . . . Chicago and its saloons and its slums fade away. . . . They behold home landscapes and childhood scenes returning; old loves and friendships begin to waken."

NOTE: Sinclair's Use of Music Watch the way Sinclair uses music to foreshadow and underscore his points here. "This scene must be read, or said, or sung, to music," Sinclair writes. The guests are inspired and transported by the irrepressible playing of Tamoszius, the first violin. But a counterpoint to the frenetic violin is the sound of the cello: "one long-drawn and lugubrious note after another."

Thus Sinclair reminds us that the party has two moods—one gay and one sad. As the party reaches its lowest point, the band switches from Lithuanian music to a "merciless" American pop tune.

Reality intrudes when Dede Antanas, Jurgis's father, rises to speak. His work in the damp, cold "pickle rooms at Durham's"—a meat-packing concern—has brought back an old respiratory disease, and he can barely talk without coughing. He is convinced he is dying. His speech is more a farewell than a congratulatory message, and he leaves his listeners weeping.

The delicatessen owner, Jokubas Szedvilas, tries to cheer up the guests with a little speech. His off-color allusions to marriage's sexual pleasures delight the young men but cause Ona, who is delicate and "not quite 16," to blush.

When the dancing begins, Sinclair hints at other problems that are gnawing at these people. Among them is a generation gap between parents and children. The young prefer the two-step an American dance; the older people prefer the complicated dances they learned in Lithuania. The young affect the latest style of clothing; they wouldn't be caught dead in the clothes their elders wear—embroidered vests or bodices brought from Europe.

As Sinclair introduces us to more and more people, we see that no one is completely free. Lucija and Jokubas Szedvilas have had to mortgage their delicatessen to pay their rent. Aniele Jukniene, widowed, sick, and mother of three children, takes in washing and raises chickens on garbage. These are defeated people, Sinclair suggests; yet with heroic energy, they pour themselves into the traditional wedding feast as a way of denying their fate. "Bit by bit these poor people have given up everything else; but . . . they cannot give up the *veselija!* To do that would mean, not merely to be defeated, but to acknowledge defeat— and the difference between these two things is what keeps the world going."

A calamity befalls the newlyweds when the contributions of the guests don't add up to the expenses of the *veselija.* In Lithuania, everyone contributes what he can after dancing with the bride in a ceremony called the *acziavimas.* But in America the tradition breaks down. In "the new country, all this was changing; it seemed as if there must be some subtle poison in the air that one breathed here—it was affecting all the young men at once."

NOTE: Use of Foreign Phrases Throughout this chapter and the rest of the novel, Sinclair employs Lithuanian words and phrases for authenticity. He rarely translates the words, but instead puts them in a context that reveals their probable meaning.

Some young men fill themselves with food and drink and sneak off. Others march out defiantly. They have adopted the competitive code of jungle animals—take or be taken from, kill or be killed—that shapes the lives of every character in the novel. Jurgis considers fighting with the freeloaders but holds himself back. An optimist, Jurgis is proud of his strength (he can carry a 250-pound quarter of beef "without a stagger") and his ability to earn money. "We will pay . . . somehow," he tells Ona. "I will work harder."

Ona has heard this vow before, in Lithuania and New York, where officials had cheated them. Hearing it again gives her heart. She thinks how wonderful it is "to have a husband . . . who could solve all problems, and who was so big and strong!"

If she had spoken her thought aloud, chances are that Jurgis—naïve male chauvinist that he is—would have agreed with her. But you've read the chapter closely enough to know better. This is a new world, one they don't understand. "A rule made in the forests of Lithuania is hard to apply in the stockyards district of Chicago, with its quarter of a million inhabitants," Sinclair tells us.

Moreover, there are big bills to pay—some of them padded, like the one they expect to get from Graic-zunas, the saloon-keeper. "The saloon-keeper stood in with all the big politics men in the district."

NOTE: Muckraking   You can view *The Jungle* as a series of exposés—of child labor, rigged horse races, political graft, sexual harassment at work, dangerous working conditions, unsanitary housing, unfair labor practices, real estate fraud, vote fraud, and so on. In this chapter Sinclair uncovers the way saloon-keepers cheat their customers, the way workers suffer when their employers take no responsibility for on-the-job injuries and the way workers are unfairly penalized for lateness. He explores these themes in depth in later chapters.

Sinclair has plunged a knife into this *veselija,* and as the chapter ends, he gives the knife a little twist. It is three o'clock in the morning. Everyone except Ona is "literally burning alcohol." Yet the dancers still move across the floor, unable to stop, to let go of the moment, the release that the day has given them. The music has changed, from Old World tunes to a popular American song. Soon—in four hours—all will be dancing to another "American tune"—the packers'— at work.

If they fail to show up, they will lose their jobs to members of "the hungry mob that waits every morning at the gates of the packing houses." Even Ona has been unable to persuade her boss at Brown's, one of the largest packing houses, to give her a day off.

Jurgis feels confident enough to flout her boss. He carries Ona—"small for her age, a mere child"—the two blocks from the saloon to their home. "You will not go to Brown's today," he tells her.

Ona has spent the night in alternating states of excitement and terror. She gasps, but Jurgis insists. "Leave it to me," he says. "I will earn more money—I will work harder."

Is this just macho bluster on Jurgis's part? Or does he really believe that hard work will be enough to ensure their survival in this harsh new world? As the story unfolds, Sinclair will spell out his own view, too. Chapter 1 has already given you a pretty good idea of what that view is.

NOTE: Stylistic Techniques Notice how Sinclair shifts tenses—from past to present, twice—as a way of putting you *in* the action much of the time. Also note the occasional inverted phrase ("Most fearful they are to contemplate, the expenses of this entertainment."). Now and then, Sinclair tries to mimic the speech patterns of the immigrants as a way of getting you to share their point of view. How well do these techniques work for you?

CHAPTER 2

Here Sinclair begins five chapters of *flashbacks*. Their purpose is to fill you in on the events that led up to the wedding, to contrast the Old World with the New, and to help you understand what motivates some of the characters, especially Jurgis.

NOTE: Plot vs. Story The chronological story Sinclair has to tell actually begins in the third paragraph of this chapter. The plot is not chronological; it doesn't present events in the order in which they happened.

Why not? A good storyteller is a tease. He sets up a problem—in this case, "Will hard work help Jurgis and Ona beat the odds?"—then in bits and pieces gives you the clues you need to solve the problem. Ideally, each clue should whet your appetite for another. A nonchronological plot helps add to the suspense.

The chapter opens with three transitional paragraphs which ease us into Jurgis's past life. We learn the answer to our question about Jurgis's sincerity immediately. He really does believe that his ability to work—and work hard—sets him apart from other men. And four months in America has only increased this young giant's belief in his own invincibility. When he hears about men who have been broken by their jobs, he just laughs. "He could not even imagine how it would feel to be beaten." So far, his strength and agility have been in such demand—he was hired at Brown's after only a half hour's wait—he can't believe anyone would "let" him starve.

The comments of the men who hear him boast are a key to his character—and to the structure of the novel from here on out. They realize that he's simply naive and inexperienced—that he has come "from very far in the country."

NOTE: **The Naïf**   What Sinclair is doing is creating in Jurgis a classic literary type called a naïf, a simple, inexperienced person who, in the course of a story has his blinders knocked off by a series of calamities. Mark Twain's Huck Finn is a naïf, and so is Voltaire's Candide. We expect such a hero to emerge from his experiences sadder but wiser, with a deeper understanding of himself and his world. But there is no guarantee that even a naïf will find wisdom.

Jurgis's listeners in Chicago had hit the nail right on the head. Jurgis had been brought up in a clearing in the middle of the Imperial Forest in Lithuania. More than a country bumpkin, he was literally, a babe in the woods. A year and a half before the wedding, he had ventured out of the forest to sell a couple of his father's horses. There he had met Ona, then 14 years old—about 11 years his junior. Jurgis is so naïve that he asks her father, "a rich man," to sell her to him for two horses. Ona's father turns Jurgis down.

When Jurgis returns a few months later, Ona's father has died, and his farm has been sold to satisfy creditors. Ona is drawn to Jurgis but won't marry him because of her love for her stepmother, Elzbieta. Elzbieta's brother Jonas, "a dried-up little man," suggests that they go to America, where a friend of his had become highly successful.

The idea appeals to Jurgis. "He would go to America and marry, and be a rich man in the bargain." And if he failed to become rich? No matter. "In that country, rich or poor, a man was free, it was said; he did not have to go into the army, he did not have to pay out his money to rascally officials—he might do as he pleased, and count himself as good as any other man."

By putting these thoughts in the mind of a naïf, Sinclair is telling us how to judge them. They are false hopes destined to be shattered. "If one could only manage to get the price of a passage," Jurgis thinks, "he could count his troubles at an end." Sinclair seems to be setting Jurgis up for disappointment.

Note how Jurgis gets the money for his passage. He spends a winter building a railroad in Smolensk—"a fearful experience, with filth and bad food and cruelty and overwork." "When they paid him off he dodged the company gamblers and dramshops [bars], and so they tried to kill him; but he escaped."

This episode is worth thinking about for two reasons. It's the first glimpse we get of "jungle" life under capitalism. (Russia would remain firmly capitalistic for another 17 years.) Even on his way home, Jurgis has to sleep "always with one eye open," on the lookout for predators. Second, the passage suggests that Sinclair's argument is not with America but with an economic system—one that can be found anywhere.

Chicago, where "Jonas's friend had gotten rich," nearly overwhelms the newcomers. There are 12 of them: Jurgis, Dede Antanas, Jonas, Ona, Marija (Ona's cousin, who is twenty years old), and Elzbieta and her six children. They spend their first night in a police station. The next morning they are taught a new word, "stockyards," and put aboard a trolley headed there.

The trolley ride further foreshadows the fate that awaits them. The buildings in the promised land are "ugly and dirty." Smoke pollutes the air and earth and darkens the sky. As they approach Packingtown, fields become "parched and yellow, the landscape hideous and bare." Everywhere, there's a "strange, pungent odor." They can't place it. "It was an elemental odor, raw and crude"—very like the smell of the jungle.

When they arrive at the stockyards, they notice chimneys belching smoke that "might have come from the center of the world." They are disturbed by an "elemental" sound—the lowing and grunting of thousands of cattle and pigs in the distance.

By chance, they pass the delicatessen owned by Jokubas Szedvilas, "the mythical friend who had made his fortune in America." Jokubas becomes their mentor and guide and sends them to the home of the widow Aniele Jukniene. Her filthy four-room flat is full of lodgers, anywhere from six to fourteen people in a room. It's the worst accommodation Jurgis and his extended family have seen in all their travels, but they make do.

Jurgis has already been disabused of one preconception. The high prices have made him realize he will not get rich, a letdown not made any easier by the fact that they're spending the money they brought with them faster than expected.

But again Jurgis is irrepressible. "Tomorrow," he says matter-of-factly, "I will get a job, and perhaps Jonas will get one also; and then we can get a place of our own."

Jurgis and Ona go for a walk, giving Sinclair a chance to do some muckraking. The houses have been built on land "made" out of a city dump. The stench is overpowering, suggesting "all the dead things of the universe." Along the neglected roadways, children play in potholes "full of stinking green water." In a dump site that's still being filled, other children rake through garbage.

Ona and Jurgis aren't dismayed. Characteristically, they are impressed at the efficient way the land is used; to build bricks, a brick company had excavated the land now used for the dump. Nearby is another hole full of polluted, "festering" water that in wintertime will be sold as ice.

What is this awful place they're in? The belching chimneys and the smell of death suggest it may be hell. To emphasize the metaphor, Sinclair evokes some satanic imagery. At sunset, "the sky in the West turned blood red, and the tops of the houses shone like fire."

But do Jurgis and Ona make the connection? Of course not. They're looking away from the sunset, toward Packingtown! And the sunset light is playing tricks on them. The smoke which had this afternoon been so frightening is now multicolored. In the twilight the great packinghouses offer "a vision of power . . . a dream of wonder, with its tale of human energy . . . of opportunity and freedom, of life and love and joy."

Misreading all the clues as usual, Jurgis feels a surge of confidence. "Tomorrow," he says, "I shall go there and get a job!"

NOTE: **Shifting Point of View** Sinclair's narrators often step forward and lectures us about subjects his characters can know little or nothing about. We get a glimpse of that habit in the last scene, when he muckrakes about the dump or explains how unhealthy water is sold as ice in winter.

This shifting point of view may bother readers who prefer narrators to stay close to their characters and make discoveries with them. Remember, though, that Sinclair has chosen to play several roles: dramatizer, muckraker, historian, and pamphleteer. He often changes roles abruptly, sounding like a novelist in one line and an outraged magazine writer in the next. If these changes disturb you, they are probably too abrupt, a flaw in Sinclair's technique.

CHAPTER 3

The flashback continues the next day as Jokubas takes the newcomers on a tour of Packingtown—the stockyards and packinghouses. The tour gives Sinclair a chance to introduce some metaphors that make turn-of-the-century Chicago such an ideal setting for *The Jungle*.

In the morning, one of the bosses at Brown's picks Jurgis out of the crowd of jobseekers and tells him to start the next day. So the outing afterwards is a celebration, making Jurgis even more resistant than usual to negative interpretations of what he sees and hears.

Jokubas is an ebullient guide. Sinclair is wearing his historian's hat through much of this chapter and lets Jokubas spout the data he (Sinclair) had gathered on the stockyard operations. We learn that the plants

"process" about 30,000 animals a day, that in the cattle pens there are 25,000 gates, and in the stockyards,
250 miles of railroad track. These are the sort of facts
public relations people drum up to impress outsiders,
and they make their mark. When Jokubas rattles them
off, "his guests cry out with wonder," and Jurgis
swells with pride. "Had he not . . . become a sharer in
all this activity, a cog in this marvelous machine?"

The pace, efficiency, and size of the packing-house
operations leave him awestruck.

NOTE: Allegory of the Hogs   When a writer
tells the story through *symbols*—using animals, for
instance, to stand for human beings—he is said to be
speaking allegorically. `Sinclair creates this kind of
symbolic narrative by suggesting that the hogs, who
climb the chutes leading to their deaths "by the power
of their own legs," are like the immigrants who flock
to Packingtown.

Read this passage closely. Note the many compar-
isons between hogs and humans. Some readers think
Sinclair goes overboard with the analogy when he
talks of "the hog-squeal of the universe" and a "god of
hogs, to whom this hog-personality was precious."
But in this allegory is an echo of *The Jungle*'s major
theme: Industrial capitalism—an efficient, impersonal
"slaughtering machine"—sacrifices its workers in a
horrible way.

The group visits the place where cattle are slaughtered—and watches men on the "killing bed" work
"with furious intensity, literally on the run." The half-
inch pool of blood they work in "must have made the
floor slippery, but no one could have guessed this by
watching the men at work."

What you see, Sinclair hints, is not what you get—whether you are a worker or a consumer. "The visitors did not see any more than the packers wanted them to," Jokubas whispers. He translates signs demanding cleanliness, while offering to take his guests "to the secret rooms where the spoiled meats went to be doctored." He points out a government inspector assigned to inspect hog carcasses for tuberculosis. A "sociable person," Jokubas explains, might divert the inspector's attention while "a dozen carcasses were passing untouched."

To Jurgis, it is almost sacrilegious to speak with skepticism of the Beef Trust (the several companies that made up Chicago's packing industry)—"a thing as tremendous as the universe." The big plants "were really all one," Jokubas confides. (Readers in 1906 would have interpreted that phrase as an accusation that the owners of the big packinghouses conspired to fix prices, keep wages low, and smother competition.

Jurgis becomes a convert to the view that the laws and ways of Packingtown (or, more broadly, Big Business) are not to be questioned or understood any more readily than the universe, "that this whole huge establishment had taken him under its protection, and had become responsible for his welfare."

The chapter ends with a wicked allusion to the Sherman Anti-Trust Act of 1890, which supposedly outlawed concentrations of economic power such as the Beef Trust. Sinclair refers to it as the "law of the land" that requires the meat packers "to be deadly rivals" and encourages them "to ruin each other under penalty of fine and imprisonment!" It's a law, Sinclair suggests, that sanctions the predatory order of the jungle by insisting on competitive practices. As you will see later on, Sinclair wants to substitute cooperation for competition in economic life.

NOTE: Advertising Signs   Eighty years ago,
when our consumer economy was just finding its
legs, advertisements could be as distracting as they
are today. Note how Sinclair, almost as an aside, rails
against "placards that defaced the landscape," "silly
little jingles," and "gaudy pictures." Chapter 5 will
open with a more light-hearted assault on the adver-
tiser's art. Chapter 31 contains an economic argument
against advertising.

CHAPTER 4

This chapter gives Sinclair a chance to show how
easily newly arrived immigrants can be taken in by
people determined to defraud them. And it gives you
a chance to study how a writer can communicate
panic and tension by stepping up the pace of his narrative.

Sinclair begins by describing Jurgis's first day on the
killing beds, sweeping entrails into a trap in the floor.
He is delighted with the money he earns—17½ cents
an hour, more than $1.50 for the 12-hour day. Back at
Aniele's lodging house, there's a celebration, because
Jonas and Marija have been offered jobs. Marija will
be doing skilled piecework, painting cans. Jonas will
push a hand truck at Durham's.

Jurgis has decided that the older children will go to
school and that Elzbieta and Ona will stay home to
keep house. Dede Antanas—too old for a job in
America, Jurgis is told—has spent two days seeking
work, with no luck. The packers discard men once
they grow old, Jokubas explains. His comment under-
lines the novel's theme that capitalist industries wear
out their workers, then turn away from them.

An advertisement for a house catches Jurgis's eye and persuades the family to consider buying their own home. They're easy marks for the smooth-talking real estate agent. Just how easy, Sinclair makes clear in a detailed account of the negotiations that lead up to the purchase. Jurgis, who is illiterate, can't calculate how much they'll need to make the monthly payments. Luckily, "Ona was like lightning at such things." The dingy one-story house, which the agent is trying to pawn off as new, is full of defects, but the peasant family "tried to shut their eyes" to them.

Jokubas warns them not to buy. He's seen too many people "done to death in this 'buying a home' swindle." But the family is desperate—they must move somewhere. Besides, Jurgis tells himself, "others might have failed at it, but he was not the failing kind—he would show them how to do it. He would work all day, and all night, too, if need be."

Since Jurgis can't get a day off, he sends Ona and Elzbieta with Jokubas to sign the deed and make the down payment. But Jokubas, worldly as he is compared to the others, can't make any sense of the contract. It seems to provide only for the renting of the property—$12 a month for eight years.

From here to the end of the chapter, watch Sinclair speed up his story to make you feel the panic of the bewildered peasants. A lawyer who is on a first-name basis with the agent assures them that "it was all perfectly regular." Elzbieta makes the $300 down payment, and the women go home "with a deadly terror gnawing at their souls." Jurgis hears their tale and rushes out to find another lawyer, who reads the deed and explains that all is in order. So long as they make all the payments, the house will be theirs. Jurgis is so relieved, that he can't see that the hurdle of regular payments may be impossibly high. Back at Aniele's, everything is in an uproar; the women thought he had left to murder the agent. Overwhelmed by tension, Ona and Elzbieta sob themselves to sleep.

CHAPTER 5

NOTE: The Summary Narrative Approach   Sinclair handles this chapter differently than the last half of Chapter 4. There, he dramatized the action, using scenes and dialogue to give it life before our eyes. Here, he merely sums up the action with descriptive passages. Some readers welcome the change of pace. It gives them a chance to catch their breaths and provide a "kicking-off point" for the next dramatic surge. Besides, they say, Sinclair sounds at times like a textbook writer, because *The Jungle* covers so much ground.

Other readers feel that Sinclair relies too heavily on the techniques of summary narrative. In so doing, they say, he keeps the action and the characters at a distance, making it hard for us to identify with them.

Sinclair begins this chapter by poking fun at the type of advertisements that so annoyed him in Chapter 3. He ends with Jurgis "having begun to see at last how those might be right who had laughed at him for his faith in America."

On the "advice" of an advertisement, the family falls into another trap of the capitalist jungle—buying household furnishings on the installment plan. Too absorbed with the "never-ending delight" of fixing up their house, they don't notice how the debt increases their vulnerability to economic catastrophe.

On the job, Jurgis is still a naïf. The bosses keep the
men working at a frantic pace by "speeding up the
gang," but he doesn't mind. He likes being kept busy
and can't understand why the union should try to
slow the pace to protect the men who can't keep up.
Without knowing it, Jurgis shares the classic capitalist
belief in laissez faire—the freedom to succeed or fail in
economic life without interference.

And yet, his father's failure so far to find a job troubles him. Why, Jurgis wonders, are the old people
shunned in industrial America?

This "crack in the fine structure of Jurgis's faith in
things as they are" widens when he hears about a job
offer for Antanas. Someone at Durham's has promised him a job for a price: one-third of his pay. Tamoszius Kuszleika, the amateur violinist who led the
musicians at the wedding feast, explains to Jurgis that
"such cases of petty graft" are common.

NOTE: Tamoszius's View of Industry   Tamoszius's description of the way the plants are run reflects
Sinclair's dour view of industrial organization. ". . .
from top to bottom the place was simply a seething
cauldron of jealousies and hatreds; there was no loyalty or decency anywhere about it, there was no place
in it where a man counted for anything against a dollar." The place is a jungle, where even "men of the
same rank were pitted against each other."

What a horrible job Antanas gets. Sinclair puts on
his muckraker's hat and tells how Antanas earns his
money cleaning the pickle (chemical) room. The
chemicals for curing canned beef are reused no matter
how contaminated they get, and the meat sludge that
gets caught in the drains is retrieved for canning.
Antanas is unwillingly part of a conspiracy to cheat

and possibly endanger the health of consumers. And
so is Jurgis in his job, when he helps process unborn
calves and cattle that have died on the way to the
slaughterhouse.

This discovery is a major blow to Jurgis's "faith in
America." So is the news that Marija owes her job to
the boss's decision to fire a mother who took sick and
that Jonas replaced a worker injured on the job. Like
vultures, they are profiting from others' misfortunes.
Sinclair has begun to knock the blinders from Jurgis's
eyes.

CHAPTER 6

Sinclair continues the education of Jurgis by revealing how real estate agents take advantage of the poor
and by beginning an exposé of child labor. All this
may not sound like the stuff of fiction to you. But
notice how carefully Sinclair integrates the facts and
figures of his research into the story.

"Jurgis judged everything by the criterion of its
helping or hindering their union." He's losing his
naiveté; yet for Ona's sake he's willing to stand any
hardship and overlook "the tricks and cruelties he
saw at Durham's."

He and Ona want to forego tradition and get married at once, but Elzbieta won't hear of it. So they
postpone the event until they can raise money for the
wedding feast.

A visit from Grandmother Majauszkiene, a wise old
neighbor, brings them the bad news that they've been
swindled. The house is not new; at least four families
have lived there before and were evicted when they
missed payments. Moreover, the true monthly payments are $17, not $12. No one had told them about
the interest! "You are like the rest," the old lady says,
"they trick you and eat you alive"—like animals in a
real jungle.

Jurgis swears to "work harder," but for the first time he begins to realize that the forces arrayed against him are more powerful than he. Ona gets a job sewing covers on hams after bribing the forelady. Elzbieta finds a priest to certify that Stanislovas, her oldest son, is 16—two years beyond his true age. Armed with his certificate, Stanislovas gets a job at Durham's filling cans with lard.

Stanislovas isn't the only child in America who must go to work instead of school. He's one of almost two million children working for about 50 cents a day, six days a week.

At the chapter's end, Sinclair returns to the young lovers. Ona and Jurgis "have calculated that the added income leaves "them just about as they had been before!"

NOTE: Characterization of Grandmother Majauszkiene The old lady is an interesting figure, partly because she is the first socialist we meet. Sinclair portrays her as a witch—"unrelenting, typifying fate." And so she appears to the family. She "had lived in the midst of misfortune so long that it had come to be her element, and she talked about starvation, sickness, and death as other people might about weddings and holidays."

Like Shakespeare's witches, she can foretell the future. Note, especially, her remark that their house is unlucky, that someone is bound to get consumption. This prophecy will come true in the next chapter.

CHAPTER 7

After a transitional paragraph, the flashback ends, and the story picks up after the wedding feast in Chapter 1. More than $100 in debt, Ona and Jurgis must begin their married life with the ".lash of want" cracking over their heads.

Jurgis resolves to protect Ona "against the horror he saw about them." And yet he fails when Ona, too poor to own a raincoat, gets sick after a drenching downpour. (In a mini-exposé, Sinclair lays part of the blame on the greed of the men who own the trolley lines.)

The rest of the chapter is a laundry list of the dangers strewn in the family's path: advertisements and companies that lie, the cesspool beneath the house, "doctored" foods, low-quality winter clothes, bedbugs and roaches.

Antanas can't stop coughing. He's the consumptive that Grandmother Majauszkiene warned about. He dies, and Jurgis, wiser now, negotiates a bargain funeral.

The "dreadful winter" joins the list of dangers. Workers sicken and are replaced by "starving, penniless men" lined up for work outside the packing plants. Sinclair compares the ailing workers to the "weaker branches" that are knocked off forest trees by winter storms. The message is clear: Only the fittest will survive the winter in Packingtown.

NOTE: The Metaphor of Natural Selection
With his image of the tree, Sinclair is making a reference to the theories of Charles Darwin, the English naturalist. Darwin's theory of evolution holds that all species continually struggle to survive. The species with the best chance for survival, he felt, are those most able to adapt to their environment. Species that are the least fit fail to reproduce, and die out.

The French writer, Émile Zola, was fascinated by Darwin's theories and structured his novels to "prove" some of those ideas. Readers who feel that

The Jungle is a Naturalist novel structured like Zola's cite this chapter to prove their case.

Other readers say that Sinclair used Darwinism and Zolaist techniques only when they served his purposes—as they do, clearly, in this chapter. Darwinism is an apt metaphor for the process of selection that takes place in Packingtown during the winter months. And it allows Sinclair to foreshadow the fate of Ona, who "was not fitted for a life as this."

Conditions at the plants are pitiful. Men on the killing floor are hobbled by the blood that turns to ice on their feet. Those in the cooking rooms—the only place in the plant that's warm—run the risk of catching cold when they "pass through ice-cold corridors."

Another winter danger is the saloons on "Whiskey Row." They lure customers by providing essential services for the poor workers: warmth, check-cashing, a place to eat near the plants.

In the poetic passage that ends the chapter, Sinclair personifies the cold, "a living thing, a demon presence." If you've ever been really cold, you'll understand how the cold can be "yelling out" or be still as death "as it crept in through the cracks, reaching out for them with its icy, death-dealing fingers."

CHAPTER 8

This chapter is a turning point for Jurgis. His family's fortunes sink when a slump in the meat-packing business occurs. Disillusioned, he joins the union, "for he understood that a fight was on, and that it was his fight."

Before introducing this crisis, Sinclair trots out the elfin musician, Tamoszius, for a bit of comic relief. He falls in love with Marija when he discovers that, despite her booming voice and violent energy, she has "the heart of a baby." He proposes marriage; she accepts; and they plan a spring wedding.

But their love is doomed. With the holiday season over, consumer demand is low, so Marija's canning factory shuts down until business improves.

The slowdown affects the entire industry. Jurgis has to report to work each day at seven but is paid only when cattle are processed—for weeks on end, no more than two hours a day. He is never paid "broken time"—fractional parts of hours.

The injustice makes a union man of him. This is his second conversion. (The first, in Chapter 3, was to Big Business.) Soon all the working members of his family wear union buttons. Yet they can't understand why the union can't prevent Marija's factory from closing. Unions don't fare well in this novel—the packers are quicker, stronger, more flexible.

Toward the end of the chapter, Sinclair puts another clown on stage—Tommy Finnegan. Finnegan corners Jurgis at a union meeting and rattles on in an Irish brogue about the world of the spirits. The entire confrontation takes no more than a paragraph but is worth noting, because it shows Sinclair's talent for creating memorable characters in only a few words.

CHAPTER 9

This complicated chapter begins with Jurgis in night school and ends with a worker being rendered into lard. It gives you an opportunity to study the narrator as he switches in and out of several guises: storyteller, historian, muckraker. Throughout, Sinclair resorts to summary narrative, the most efficient way to cover so much territory.

Jurgis's union activities have inspired him to learn to speak and read English. At the same time, he begins groping with political concepts. The union begins to show him what a democracy can be.

In a brief flashback, Sinclair indicates how true democracy has been corrupted in America. A night watchman at Durham's helps him become naturalized so that he can vote. On election day, the watchman then pays him $2 to vote Democratic.

All this is done with the complicity of business interests and the police. That complicity reinforces Sinclair's theme that business and government work hand-in-hand to corrupt the democratic process. Durham's gives Jurgis a half-day off, with pay, to become naturalized, and two hours off to vote. At the polling place, a cop makes sure Jurgis marks his ballot the way he was told.

Friends in the union help him make sense of these transactions, with a distorted picture of the way our democratic system works. "The officials who ruled [the government], and got all the graft, had to be elected first; and so there were two rival sets of grafters, known as political parties, and the one got the office which bought the most votes."

Sinclair, the muckraker, gives a scathing portrait of Mike Scully, boss of Chicago's Democratic machine. Scully boasts he is "the people's man," but he's only interested in money and power. He has plenty of both, largely due to his position as patronage chief and intermediary between the city government and the packers.

Sinclair lists some of the packers' crimes: stealing city water, selling condemned meat in Illinois, adulterating foods, mislabeling canned goods. He describes the occupational diseases and injuries that threaten packing-house workers: amputated thumbs, tuberculosis in the cooking rooms, men unable to stand straight, fingers eaten off by acid, rheumatism, and more. The list ends with Sinclair's most sensational revelation: men tumbling into cooking vats and being rendered into lard.

Theodore Roosevelt's investigators, checking up on Sinclair's allegations, could find no proof of the man-into-lard story. But it doesn't matter. It was the metaphor Sinclair was after. Figuratively, if not literally, the workers' lives were being destroyed and eaten by the world.

NOTE: Use of Literary Allusions   Sinclair read widely, and he tends to litter *The Jungle* with references to his favorite books and authors. For instance, he says that a cattle butcher's descriptions of diseased cattle "would have been worthwile for a Dante or Zola."

Dante Alighieri (1265–1321) depicted Hell in graphic detail in his classic poem *The Divine Comedy*. Émile Zola was famous for his unflinchingly realistic descriptions of the seamy side of everyday life.

Some readers have raised objections to these allusions on the grounds that they are out of character. For example, the illiterate Jurgis would never have drawn a connection between Dante, Zola, and the butcher. Once more, Sinclair has simply stepped into the story to interpret events for us as Sinclair, not as one of his characters.

CHAPTER 10

Sinclair moves ahead with his story, focusing on the family's domestic life. Marija's factory is still closed. Jurgis is earning only about half his regular wages. Worry and fear stalk the family; they're not sure why. "They were willing to work all the time; and when people do their best, ought they not be able to keep alive?"

Trapped in a consumer economy, "There never seemed to be an end to the things they had to buy." Insurance on the house, taxes, water fees—Jurgis pried this bad news out of the agent.

Spring comes, then summer. Sinclair addresses you directly, forcing you to compare your summer pleasures with the grueling routines of "men and women and children who . . . never saw any green thing, not even a flower."

Workers can never forget that they are on the bottom. "People who worked with their hands were a class apart, and were made to feel it." When Sinclair makes a statement like that, you can be sure he'll find a plot twist to prove it. Sure enough, Marija's canning factory opens, but she "forgets her place" and loses her job. Her crime was to challenge the supervisor for not crediting her with work she had done. In time, she gets a job trimming beef at half her earlier wage. But she has been hurt and made to recognize her own vulnerability.

Marija's fate is an unfortunate object lesson for Ona. Ona is having problems with her forelady, Miss Henderson, who, as a sideline, recruits Ona's co-workers for a brothel. Prostitution and sexual harassment are rampant in Packingtown. Sinclair compares the harassment with the situation that existed "under the system of chattel slavery." Yet in Packingtown, there is "no difference in color between master and slave."

It's an ominous clue, this comparison between wage slaves and chattel slaves. Ona is not a strong person. How will she resist her "brutal and inscrupulous" masters if they demand sexual favors? Especially now, when Marija's experience has taught Ona not to "forget her place"?

Ona has a baby which they name after Jurgis's father. Little Antanas makes Jurgis "irrevocably a family man." And yet the baby brings pain, too—an awareness of how little freedom workers have to enjoy their children.

As for Ona, the family's needs require her to return to work after only a week at home. The lack of rest leads to "womb trouble," and Sinclair is careful to show that Ona's is not an isolated case. "The great majority of women . . . in Packingtown suffered in the same way, and from the same cause."

CHAPTER 11

Sinclair is impatient to make his case against capitalism. He rushes on, relentlessly summarizing the action, pausing for a welcome line of dialogue at the end of the chapter.

The packers expect a strike and are eager to create a pool of trained workers to replace the strikers. So they take on more hands than they need, denying Jurgis overtime and thus reducing his pay. Meanwhile, the speed-ups continue.

Winter comes, and Jurgis fights a blizzard to get to work. In his triumph, Jurgis is like "some monarch of the forest that has vanquished his foe." But he has an accident at work and the company refuses to accept responsibility. Confined to bed, he can no longer contribute to his family's welfare. Ona draws money out of their tiny savings account, and they make do.

Only little Antanas can distract Jurgis. Jurgis says, in a line of dialogue that brings him alive for us,

"Look, Muma, he knows his papa! He does, he does!
Tu mano szirdele, the little rascal!"

CHAPTER 12

Like Marija, Jurgis is forced to confront his own
limits. He returns to work and hobbles through the
day. When the pain won't let him finish, he weeps
"like a child." A doctor orders him to bed for two
months. Finally, in April he shows up for work only
to discover that his job has been given to another
man.

There is no work for him anywhere, and he realizes
why. "They had got the best out of him—they had
worn him out, with their speeding up and their care-
lessness, and now they had thrown him away!"

It's a common plight. Jurgis meets other unemployed men and finds "that they had all had the same
experience. . . . The vast majority . . . were simply the
worn-out parts of the great merciless packing machine."

Elzbieta's brother, Jonas, disappears—probably
"gone on the road, seeking happiness." Vilimas, age
11, and Nikalojus, age 10, are pulled out of school and
sent to sell newspapers. They become streetwise and
ride trolleys without paying. They too are sinking into
the ways of the jungle—learning to take before being
taken.

CHAPTER 13

The family slides deeper and deeper into the "social
pit." Kristoforas, one of Elzbieta's two crippled children, dies suddenly—probably poisoned by a sausage he ate. Elzbieta begs money from neighbors for a
proper funeral.

Desperate, Jurgis takes a job at the fertilizer plant, a
place so horrible men talk about it "in whispers." The
plant's foul odor clings to Jurgis and makes him an
outcast.

Vilimas and Nikalojus have adapted too well to
their environment to suit Jurgis. They learn to swear,
smoke, and gamble; and often they sleep downtown
in doorways to save transit time. So it is decided that
Kotrina, who is 13, will take care of the house, Elzbieta
will get a job, and the boys will return to school.

Sinclair gives a detailed description of Elzbieta's job
as "a servant to a 'sausage machine.' " She sits in a
damp cellar amid "a sickening odor of moist flesh,"
twisting sausages into links. She is so busy, she has
no time to look up at the gallery, from which visitors
"stare at her, as at some wild beast in a menag-
erie."

CHAPTER 14

This chapter is partly an exposé of the "spoiled-
meat industry" and partly an examination of the general gloom that has settled over the Rudkus household.

Elzbieta becomes an example of the theme that the
poor often work against their best interests. She now
makes the type of sausage that may have killed Kristoforas. Among the ingredients are spoiled and doctored meat; dirt, sawdust, and tuberculosis germs; rat
dung, rat poison, and even the rats themselves! No
wonder *The Jungle* outraged Americans in 1906!

A pall has fallen over the family. The adults rarely
talk to each other. All they have to look forward to are
six punishing years before they're free of house payments. As for Ona and Jurgis, "their moods so seldom

came together. . . . It was as if their hopes were buried in separate graves."

Jurgis starts to drink to ease his pain. But he stops when he sees his family's despair. From then on, nearly every moment "consisted of a struggle with the craving for liquor."

We do not see the struggle, of course, because Sinclair does not dramatize it. Yet we are told about it convincingly, perhaps because Sinclair had seen drunkenness in his own home. (His father died from alcoholism a month after *The Jungle* appeared.)

Ona is pregnant again and "visibly going to pieces." She has a cough—the fear is of consumption.

CHAPTER 15

Two similes from the animal world crop up in the first paragraph to remind us of the symbolism suggested by the book's title. Ona has a look in her eye that seems to Jurgis "like the eye of a hunted animal." Jurgis "lives like a dumb beast of burden."

He worries about Ona's frequent outbreaks. She's holding back "some terrible thing"; he's sure of it.

Just before Thanksgiving, Ona fails to come home. It was the snowstorm, she explains the next morning. It stopped the trolleys, so she stayed with a friend, Jadvyga Marcinkus.

A month later Ona again fails to come home. Jurgis goes to Jadvyga's, but Ona isn't there. What's more, he learns, she never spent a night there.

He visits the place where Ona works, to speak to Ona's forelady, but Miss Henderson has not shown up. The trolley lines from downtown haven't been working since the previous night.

In the afternoon, Jurgis heads home and spots Ona on a trolley. He watches her enter their house, then follows. Ona confesses that she spent the night at Miss Henderson's. Jurgis knows that Henderson lives in a brothel with Phil Connor, head of the loading gang.

Enraged, he nearly strangles Ona. She explains that Connor had threatened that her family would lose their jobs unless she submitted to him. Then he raped her and forced her to visit the brothel with him.

Ona knows what Jurgis will do. "You will kill him—and we shall die."

Jurgis takes off "breathing hoarsely, like a wounded bull." At the yards, he finds his prey and lunges for "the great beast." A dozen men drag him off, and he is arrested. But Jurgis has the passion of a jungle animal. He has sunk "his teeth into the man's cheek; and when they tore him away he was dripping with blood, and little ribbons of skin were hanging in his mouth."

Sinclair's dramatization of the events in this chapter is a welcome change from so many chapters of straight summary narrative.

CHAPTER 16

In this chapter Sinclair will announce another turning point for Jurgis—"the beginning of his rebellion, of his outlawry and his unbelief." He will also portray American justice as "a sham and a loathsome mockery."

When he is booked for assault and battery, Jurgis is careful not to provoke the police. The lions of the jungle, their station house is "their inmost lair." "It was as much a man's very life was worth to anger them."

In his cell, Jurgis wrestles with his conscience. He realizes he has made things worse for Ona and little Antanas and blames himself for not protecting her from "a fate which every one knew to be so common." She will never get over her adultery, he fears. "The shame of it would kill her." It's a blunt foreshadowing of her fate.

In the morning Jurgis is arraigned in front of the notorious Justice Callahan. Callahan's nickname, "Growler" Pat, labels him a jungle dweller. Sinclair uses a vivid metaphor to tell us once again that American justice is in the service of business: "If Scully was the thumb, Pat Callahan was the first finger of the unseen hand whereby the packers held down the people of the district."

A company lawyer asks Callahan to hold Jurgis for a week. Callahan quickly orders Jurgis held on $300 bail—almost a year's wage!

His first night at the county jail Jurgis can't sleep. He paces "like a wild beast that breaks its teeth on the bars of its cage."

Church bells remind him that it's Christmas Eve, and a rush of poignant memories come to mind. He rails against society, which has destroyed his life, and his family and jailed him "as if he had been a wild beast." He's still to naïve to trace his problems to the nation's competitive economic system with its attendant evils. All he knows is that "society, with all its powers, had declared itself his foe."

Imprisonment has changed his outlook. His rebellion has begun. Sinclair calls on the poet Oscar Wilde to explain why. In prison, Wilde wrote in his 1898 poem "The Ballad of Reading Gaol": "It is only what is good in Man / That wastes and withers there."

CHAPTER 17

Sinclair structures this chapter in an unusually absorbing way. He gives us three dramatic scenes—one comic, one bitter, one pathetic—and connects each scene with a passage of exposition.

Scene 1. Jurgis gets a cellmate—a dapper young safecracker named Jack Duane. Duane is Jurgis's opposite—worldly, lighthearted, and openly at war with society. After college, he had developed a telegraphic device and "been robbed of it by a great company."

NOTE: The Naturalist View of Marriage   Duane tells Jurgis that "this wasn't a world in which a man had any business with a family." This motif crops up again and again in *The Jungle*, as it does in the novels of Émile Zola, founder of the French Naturalist school of literature.

According to the Naturalists, marriage is a trap that men are forced into by their sexual urge. Jurgis once believed this. In chapter 2 we read, "Jurgis had never expected to get married—he had laughed at it as a foolish trap for a man to walk into."

It's a trap for Jurgis and other workingmen because the need to support a family makes the workingman vulnerable to all sorts of exploitation, another Sinclair theme. Duane foresees the day when Jurgis will "give up the fight and shift for himself."

Exposition. Duane regales Jurgis with his adventures and expands Jurgis's world by introducing him to other prisoners—animals in this "Noah's ark of the city's crime." (Like many metaphors, this one falls apart when you examine it too closely. The jail, unlike the ark, saves no one, although some do view it as a brief respite from the outside world.) Sinclair then switches metaphors, calling the prisoners "the drainage of the great festering ulcer of society"—an ugly symptom of an economic system that's based on greed, and a political system that is corrupt. Everything in this society is for sale, including "justice and honor, women's bodies and men's souls."

Notice how frequently Sinclair conjures up the animal world. In Chicago, "human beings writhed and fought and fell upon each other like wolves in a pit." The fighting and lusts and corruption are a "wild-beast tangle."

Sinclair defends the prisoners' nonchalant attitude toward imprisonment. Being in prison is no disgrace to them: they know that "the game had never been fair, the dice were loaded." Besides, the real criminals are "the swindlers and thieves of millions of dollars"—the packers and their henchmen.

Scene 2. Callahan tries Jurgis in court, with Elzbieta and Kotrina looking on. Through an interpreter Jurgis tries to give his side of the story, but the judge does not listen and sentences him to 30 days in jail plus court costs.

Exposition. Jurgis ends up in another jail, the Bridewell, and spends 10 days breaking stone—a welcome relief from his cellmate, a quarrelsome Norwegian sailor.

Scene 3. Stanislovas visits with the news that Jurgis's worst fears have materialized. Ona is sick. Marija can't work—her hand is gangrenous from a job injury. Elzbieta's job is gone, so she begs for food from the neighbors. Stanislovas too has lost his job and must sell newspapers with his two brothers and Kotrina. Stunned, Jurgis gives Stanislovas 14 cents—all he has in the world.

CHAPTER 18

Released from prison, Jurgis walks the twenty miles back to Chicago. Compare this trek with the trolley ride that took him and the family to Packingtown the day after they arrived in Chicago. This journey is also leading him to a new life. However, the satanic symbolism of chapter 2 is gone, and Jurgis is a different person—weary, less naîve, with fewer illusions.

Still, dangers are everywhere. Unpaved paths are "treacherous with deep slush holes." Each railroad crossing is "a death trap for the unwary." In the center of the city, sooty snow has made the streets "sewers of inky blackness, with horses slipping and plunging."

Jurgis avoids these traps only to discover the jaws of one snapped shut. His house has been repainted and sold; his family has moved back to square one—Aniele Jukniene's lodging house.

The history of their suffering rushes through Jurgis's mind. The house was a reason for their sacrifice, and now it has become a symbol of that sacrifice.

At Aniele's lodging house, Jurgis finds Ona in the throes of premature childbirth. She prays for death.

Jurgis realizes they have no doctor, no midwife. "We—we have no money," Marija whispers. He collects $1.25 from the women sitting downstairs and rushes out to find a midwife.

NOTE: Medical Care for the Poor A recurrent theme of the novel is the inadequate medical care available to the poor. Ona and her friends with "womb trouble" put their faith in patent medicines of dubious value. A cure for Kristoforas's lameness was out of reach for Elzbieta—but not for the "Chicago billionaire" who hired a "great European surgeon" to cure his daughter of the same disease. And now Ona must deal with an agonizing and dangerous birth with no medical help.

CHAPTER 19

In Madame Haupt, the midwife, Sinclair creates one of the novel's most convincing characters. Take a few moments to study the way he approaches her.

He begins dropping clues about her in the first sentence. We have an idea of her circumstances from the fact that she lives "over a saloon," at the top of a "dingy flight of steps."

When we meet her, she's "frying pork and onions" in a smoky room and drinking from a "black bottle." Sinclair describes her as "enormously fat" and dressed in "a filthy blue wrapper"; her teeth are black. With this woman as Ona's only hope, we know that Ona is going to die.

And yet, Madame Haupt is a comic figure. She is a grotesque—a clown so bizarre and repulsive that she makes us respond with nervous laughter. She is pretentious; she refers to a job as a "case." She is vain; before going out, she adjusts her black bonnet until it sits just right. She is also a glutton and a money-grubber, the very personification of greed.

Still, she has a heart. Even though Jurgis can't meet her price, she agrees to go with him because she doesn't like to think of anyone suffering.

After leading Madame Haupt to Aniele's, Jurgis goes to a saloon, where a generous saloon-keeper gives him food and drink and a dry stairway to sleep in. Near dawn, he goes to Aniele's, where the midwife blames him for not getting a doctor earlier. She speaks callously to Jurgis. Ona "vill die," she says. "Der baby is dead now."

Up in the garret, Ona recognizes Jurgis just before she dies. Kotrina returns home in the morning with three dollars she earned selling papers. Jurgis uses the money to get drunk.

CHAPTER 20

Elzbieta begs enough money from neighbors for a requiem mass for Ona. But they are too poor to bury her, and the city buries her in potter's field.

Elzbieta convinces Jurgis to stay and take care of little Antanas. Having been blacklisted, Jurgis can't get a job in Packingtown—another example of the power of the Beef Trust to control a worker's life. Blacklisting, Sinclair says, is "a warning to the men, and a means of keeping down union agitation and political discontent."

Jurgis lands a job with a farm equipment manufacturer—another giant factory, this time part of the Harvester Trust. The job allows Sinclair to shine his critic's lamp on another industry, enforcing his point is that it's the entire economic system, not just the meat-packing industry, that toys with workers' lives.

Jurgis's new job is in a modern, well-designed plant with a restaurant, a reading room, and spacious workshops. Yet the men are paid by the piece, requiring them to work at breakneck speed to earn a living. Sinclair explains all about piecework in a muckraking passage that ends: "If we are the greatest nation the sun ever shone upon, it would seem to be mainly because we have been able to goad our wage-earners to the pitch of a frenzy."

Sinclair muckrakes the trolley companies, too. This "street-car monopoly" avoids giving transfers to commuters like Jurgis, who must ride more than one line to get to work. Jurgis chooses, instead, to walk.

Jurgis's new job allows him to "pick up heart again and to make plans." But after nine days his department is closed to allow the demand for farm equipment to catch up with the supply.

CHAPTER 21

This chapter marks another turning point in Jurgis's life—he is now released from the family obligations that made it easy for bosses, politicians, and con men to use him. Before making that break complete, however, Sinclair again batters his hero with another series of psychological, physical, and economic setbacks.

Jurgis is heartbroken at his layoff from the farm equipment plant, but the experience has taught him something valuable. There's something wrong when industrialists as "enlightened" as the managers of the harvester plant can't protect their workers' jobs. "It had happened that way before, said the men, and it would happen that way forever." What Sinclair is suggesting—and Jurgis doesn't quite understand—is that the boom-bust rhythms of the capitalist economic system are absurd. The reward for a man's "doing his duty too well" during boom periods is "only to be turned out to starve" during bust periods.

Jurgis returns to the streets, "begging for any work." At night he sleeps in a police station with other homeless men. For food, he is totally dependent on Elzbieta's children, who give him a little money every day.

Another of Elzbieta's children, the crippled Juozapas, is responsible for his finding another job. While poking around Mike Scully's dump for food, Juozapas meets a settlement worker. Note Sinclair's sarcastic view of these early social workers: "rich people who came to live there to find out about the poor people." This one wears "a long fur snake around her neck" and cries on Elzbieta's shoulder at the family's tale of woe. But through her Jurgis gets a job at a steel mill in South Chicago.

Jurgis is taken on a tour of the plant. Once more, Sinclair gives a fascinating description of an industrial process. Note the poetic images Sinclair uses: Cauldrons of molten iron are "big enough for all the devils of hell to brew their broth in." "Iron bands" seize "iron prey." A steel rail is made from an ingot "the size of a man's body." "In the grip of fate," this "body" is transformed into "a great red snake escaped from purgatory." The factory seems like a torture chamber in hell. And it is here, moving rails, that Jurgis ends up.

After three weeks on the job, Jurgis one day rushes to aid fellow workers who have been splattered by molten iron, and injures his hand. The reward for his heroism? He is "laid up for eight working days without pay."

To save transportation costs, Jurgis had been living near the plant, returning to Aniele's only for Saturday night and Sunday. With his new job, however, Jurgis can spend long hours with little Antanas and delight in his growth.

With his return to work, he begins "to make plans and dream dreams" again. It's a warning: The last time he allowed himself that luxury, he lost his job at the harvester plant. This time, after a heavy rain one day while Jurgis is at work, Antanas drowns in the flooded street in front of Aniele's house.

Jurgis has hit bottom. But he has also been liberated (from the burden of family).

CHAPTER 22

The death of Ona and now of his little son Antanas triggers a crisis in Jurgis's life. No more tenderness, no more tears—signs of weakness that "had sold him into slavery!" Instead he vows to transform himself—to become a new man by purging the past from his system. He's no longer going to think of others; he's going to be selfish, like every other animal in the jungle.

How does he change? Out in the country, he waves "derisively" at a brakeman who swears at him. He takes a long bath in a deep stream. The bath is symbolic: Jurgis scours his body and his clothes to wash away the past. He commits an act of vandalism against a farmer who is rude to him. The act—ripping up more than a hundred newly planted peach trees—is symbolic, too: "It showed his mood; from now on he was fighting, and the man who hit him would get all that he gave, every time."

Now that he is on his own, he is free to refuse work. When farmers offer him full-time work, he turns them down.

Jurgis's experience as a hobo is no more unique than his other experiences. He is part of an army of "surplus labor"—men and women who migrate from one temporary job to another. The women who follow this army are prostitutes, who have sacrificed youth and beauty and been cast aside like their used-up male counterparts.

However, Jurgis is unsuccessful in crushing the caring, warm person within him. His old self triumphs over the heartless new man that he tried to will himself to be. Overcome with grief for his dead son and wife, he hides in the woods like a sick animal and weeps.

Yet there is no going back. Ona and Antanas are gone. And he is a new man, though not the heartless one he wanted to become.

CHAPTER 23

Cold weather ends Jurgis's freedom and sends him back to Chicago. He gets a job digging a tunnel for a subway freight line, part of a scheme by Chicago merchants to break the union of teamsters who haul goods above ground. The merchants have bought off city councilmen to get them to approve the plan. This is one more example of Sinclair's theme that politicians and businessmen conspire to keep workers powerless and poor. The fact that Jurgis is a party to the scheme suggests another familiar motif. In their struggle for survival, workers often unknowingly labor against their best interests.

After six weeks Jurgis ends up in the hospital with a job injury. After Christmas—the "pleasantest Christmas he had ever had in America"—he is discharged from the hospital even though he is destitute and has no place to stay. In its own way, this public institution is just as heartless as industry!

For warmth, he spends a lot of time in saloons and even visits a mission one night, suffering through a sermon on "sin and redemption." Sinclair shows his contempt for preachers: they are "part of the order established that was crushing men down and beating them." They try to save souls when what they should be saving—with jobs, food, and shelter—are bodies. After the sermon, the homeless are sent out into the snow and must wait an hour before they can go into the police station for the night.

Jurgis becomes a beggar, though not a successful one. Some of the "pros" have "comfortable homes, and families, and thousands of dollars in the banks," we're told. Compared to them, Jurgis is "a blundering amateur."

Even as a beggar, the need for warmth keeps him close to saloons. People who give him handouts are annoyed to see him dart inside a saloon. But, as Sinclair explains, there's no place else for beggars to go for cheap food or drink and a feeling of home.

CHAPTER 24

This chapter consists of two parts. The brief section is a summary of Jurgis's current understanding of the world. The second, longer part contains the book's longest dramatized scene—the story of the one "adventure" of Jurgis's life.

Jurgis now sees civilization as "a world in which nothing counted but brutal might." Wandering about the streets, darting into bars to keep warm, he feels as though he has "lost in the fierce battle of greed." In his despair, he believes there is "no place for him anywhere," and that he is "doomed to be exterminated."

And then something happens that seems at first to contradict that gloomy diagnosis. While begging, he meets Freddie Jones, the 18-year-old son of one of the big meat packers. Freddie's parents have gone abroad; he's footloose, drunk, and "a'most busted"— down to his last $2000! When he hears that Jurgis has no place to stay, he invites Jurgis home and gives him a hundred dollar bill to pay for the cab. When they reach the mansion, Freddie orders the butler, Hamilton, to pay the cabbie, so Jurgis gets to keep the $100.

Freddie is delighted to learn that Jurgis once worked for Freddie's father. Misunderstanding relations between management and labor in Packingtown, Freddie says, "Great fren's with the men, guv'ner—labor and capital, commun'ty 'f int'rests, an' all that—" That particular misunderstanding is magnified when Fredie prices everything in the dining room. We learn that his father paid $3000 for each dining room chair—more than an unskilled worker can earn at Jones & Company in six years!

Jurgis devours a meal and drinks a full bottle of champagne while Freddie looks on in wonder. He tells Jurgis about his brother's love affair and his sister's marriage to an Italian marquis. Hearing those tales, you can't help but think about the children in Jurgis's family.

When Freddie passes out, Hamilton orders Jurgis to leave. At the door, the butler wants to search him, but Jurgis won't allow it. He has taken nothing except the $100 bill. Still, keeping the money is stealing of a sort—the first Jurgis has ever done.

NOTE: A Play on Names Sinclair makes fun of Admiral George Dewey, a naval hero of the Spanish-American War, by giving his name to "a monstrous bulldog," the pet and defender of the capitalistic Jones family. This characterization must have delighted *The Jungle's* socialist readers in 1905. The only beneficiaries of the 1898 war, in their view, were the businesses that gained new markets and sources of raw materials from Spain.

These readers must have chuckled at the butler's name, too. This cantankerous servant bears the last name of Alexander Hamilton, the first Secretary of the Treasury and a strong backer of business interests.

CHAPTER 25

This chapter—divided into four dramatized scenes and three sections of largely summary narrative—is a kind of how-to on political chicanery as well as a tour of Chicago's criminal underworld. The chapter serves Sinclair's ends as propagandist and muckraker, because it shows how politics and crime are inextricably linked to each other and to legitimate business.

When Jurgis tries to change the hundred-dollar bill in a saloon, the bartender shortchanges him and Jurgis attacks him. A policeman knocks Jurgis senseless and takes him to jail.

In court the next day Jurgis tells the truth, but it does him no good. The judge sentences him to ten days in the county jail plus court costs.

Jurgis can't fathom the injustice. But Sinclair explains the situation to us: The cop regularly takes graft from the saloon owner, and the judge is indebted to the bartender, the Democratic party "henchman" who helped hustle votes to reelect him.

In jail, Jurgis meets Jack Duane once more. He realizes he has a lot in common with Duane and the other prisoners, and after he is released, he joins Duane. Their first "job" together is a street mugging during which their victim is badly hurt; this unsettles Jurgis. But to Duane, "It's a case of us or the other fellow," justifying all crime with the law of the jungle.

Soon Duane is introducing Jurgis to the "saloons and 'sporting houses,' " where Chicago's criminal elite hangs out. From this vantage point, he begins to understand how rotten the municipal government is. The city is "owned by an oligarchy of business men" and is only "nominally ruled by the people." The

business interests pay graft to everyone, from legisla-
tors and lawyers to union leaders and newspaper edi-
tors and city employees. For a price, the police permit
everything illegal, from Sunday drinking to prostitution.

A political regular named Buck Halloran gives Jurgis a glimpse of the way criminals live off the city. He
pays Jurgis $5 to pick up city paychecks for a list of
imaginary workers. Then Jurgis learns the definition
of "pull," when Halloran has Jurgis freed from jail
after he is arrested for a drunken fight. Jurgis is grate-
ful—all the more so, because, in his new status, he
doesn't want to stay among "stinking" bums at the
police station. How quickly the change! Not long ago,
Jurgis was one of those bums, fighting for a place on
the station floor.

When Jurgis becomes Mike Scully's man at Durham's, he learns how easy it is to dupe workers.
Because he fears that the unpopularity of the Democratic candidate for alderman may cause voters to
switch parties, Scully, the Democratic boss of the
stockyards district, has struck an intricate deal with
his Republican rivals. If the Republicans promise to
run no one against Scully in next year's race for alderman, Scully will back this year's Republican choice for
the post. There's one hitch: the Republican candidate
is to be one of Scully's friends.

NOTE: Jurgis and Socialism Jurgis is becoming
more aware of socialism. The Socialist party has
become a factor in Chicago politics, one Scully hopes
to counter by having Jurgis tout the Republican candidate to his fellow workers in the stockyard. Scully
seems worried that Socialists are said to be incorrupt-
ible—they can't be bought. Jurgis doesn't care one

way or the other but is willing to accept the popular view that Socialists are "the enemies of American institutions."

Jurgis's work to stem the growth of the Socialist vote reinforces one of Sinclair's familiar motifs: Workers are often ignorant of their own best interests and continually take steps to defeat them.

At Scully's behest Jurgis returns to the stockyards to drum up support among the workers for the Republican candidate, Scotty Doyle, who will "represent the workingmen." A letter from Scully gets Jurgis a job as hog trimmer at Durham's.

On election day, Jurgis spends hundreds of dollars buying votes for Doyle. He votes six times himself. When Doyle wins, Jurgis gets drunk. Is he again using alcohol to numb his conscience?

The workers celebrate too, believing that the "power of the common people" has prevailed. Sarcastically, Sinclair speaks of "this triumph of popular government."

CHAPTER 26

As the chapter begins, Jurgis is still at Durham's, able to carouse and yet save a third of his earnings. As the chapter ends, he's back on the street, an outcast once more, with only a few dollars to his name.

In this chapter, Sinclair focuses our attention on a nationwide strike by packing-house workers. Like the real strike led by the Amalgamated Meat Cutters and Butcher Workmen in 1904, this one fails. Sinclair explains his theme: Unionism is not the answer to the workers' problems, because the packers have the army of surplus labor as scabs. They have the government and its agents in their pockets. They have a natural ally in the newspapers that sway public opinion to their side. And they have the allegiance of opportunists like Jurgis, who use the strike as a chance to get ahead.

Still a naïf when it comes to choosing sides, Jurgis at first walks out with the rest of the men. He goes to see Scully about a temporary job, but Scully can't help him. Jurgis has no alternative but to become a scab and help the packers break the strike.

NOTE: The "New 'American Heroes' " Sinclair opens the fourth section of this chapter by describing Jurgis as "one of the new 'American heroes.' " Sinclair's use of the label is ironic, of course. The source— a remark by Charles Eliot of Harvard College—was familiar to Sinclair's readers in 1906. When a real butchers' strike had polarized the nation in 1904, Eliot had come out on the side of the packers and had glorified scabs as "martyrs" who deserved protection.

In his eagerness to prove Eliot wrong, Sinclair may have gone overboard. ". . . the new American hero," he says, "contained an assortment of the criminals and thugs of the city, besides Negroes and the lowest foreigners. . . . They had been attracted more by the prospect of disorder than by the big wages."

Jurgis develops most of the characteristics of scabs that Sinclair disdains. He becomes a thug, venturing outside the yards to beat up strikers. On one such outing, he joins police in breaking up a saloon and cleaning out the cash drawer.

He becomes a boss on the killing beds for $5 a day and is told he can keep the job after the strike. Workers pay him to look the other way when they commit infractions. On off hours, he gambles and drinks.

Although he gets "used to being a master of men;" he never completely loses his sense of right and wrong. He despises himself for being a scab and takes out his self-hatred on the men, driving "them until they were ready to drop with exhaustion." And when he meets Connor again, he tries to kill him. But Connor is Jurgis's nemesis—the opponent he cannot best. Jurgis gets arrested and tossed into jail.

NOTE: Sinclair's Attitude Toward Blacks Sinclair has been accused of racism for his portrayal of blacks in this chapter. Blacks are described as "stupid black Negroes"; as people who do "not want to work"; as "big buck Negroes with daggers in their boots"; as "for the first time free [of slavery and its traditions] . . . to gratify every passion; as brawlers; as practitioners of almost pagan religious rites. Those are the stereotypical views of a bigot.

What can be said in Sinclair's defense? Some readers have said he was too zealous and painted all scabs—including "the lowest foreigners"—with a dirty brush. Other readers say that Sinclair wanted to elaborate on his metaphor of the jungle. Blacks, whose ancestors were "savages in Africa," suited his purpose. He exaggerated these "savage" qualities to emphasize his theme.

Still others say we can't hold Sinclair to blame for his stereotypical thinking; he was born in Baltimore of southern parents only thirteen years after the Civil War. It was not a time or a place that encouraged a high degree of sensitivity by whites toward black people and their culture.

The counterargument, of course, is that we expect more than ordinary sensitivity from our intellectuals—especially those who champion society's out-

casts. By those standards, Sinclair's blind spot about
blacks is inexcusable.

Jurgis's frayed political connections can't save him
anymore. "His pull had run up against a bigger
pull"—Connor's. Scully is even talking about sending
Connor to the state legislature. The best Bush Harper
can do for Jurgis is to use Jurgis's savings to bail him
out of jail. After that, Jurgis must flee, for any court
will sentence him heavily for beating up Connor.

But even his pal Harper finds a way to use Jurgis.
Harper says he's helping Jurgis "for friendship's
sake." Actually, he intends to find a way to keep Jurgis's $300 bail money himself after Jurgis flees. Jurgis,
"overwhelmed with gratitude and relief," boards a
streetcar for another part of the city.

CHAPTER 27

Sinclair has put his naïf through an endless number
of tests. Jurgis is now hardened to reality. His blinders
have been knocked off. He realizes there's no escap-
ing the harshness of life in a capitalist democracy—
not as a worker, a tramp, or even a criminal. People
with power use people without power. And the powerful, too, are used; even Scully is the packers' puppet.

Sinclair is going to make that point again in this
chapter, as he begins to tie up the plot's loose ends.
Jurgis is going to discover Marija among the used,
willingly selling her body to survive.

As the chapter opens, we find Jurgis on the run. He
is once more a victim, alone, in the jungle.

It's impossible to get a job. The packers won the
strike, and about half the strikers are back on the job.
Jurgis steals food, gets some handouts at a soup

kitchen, begs some more. One night, to stay out of the rain, he ducks into a Republican rally, where the G.O.P. candidate for Vice-President is scheduled to speak.

NOTE: The Use of Irony   Notice here the way Sinclair uses irony to signal his opposition to protective tariffs (import taxes so high they keep out foreign goods): The "system of Protection" is "an ingenious device whereby the workingman permitted the manufacturer to charge him higher prices, in order that he might receive higher wages; thus taking his money out of his pocket with one hand, and putting a part of it back with the other."

Read the entire passage closely to see how Sinclair uses irony to ridicule the candidate.

The speech puts Jurgis to sleep and his snoring gets him kicked out of the rally. He starts begging and, by chance, runs into Alena Jasaityte, the "belle of the wedding feast." She gives him Marija's address.

Jurgis goes there, discovers that Marija is a prostitute, and gets caught with her in a police raid. While she dresses to go to the police station, Marija gives Jurgis news about the family. Stanislovas got locked in a room at work and was eaten by rats. Elzbieta has a job, but Marija's earnings are needed to help take care of the children. A work accident cost Tamoszius a finger, and no longer able to play the violin, he left Chicago.

What most shocks Jurgis is Marija; ". . . she was so quiet—so hard! It struck fear to his heart to watch her." Here is the woman who began the book defending "the best home traditions." Now she sees things "from the business point of view." "When people are starving," she explains, "and they have anything with a price, they ought to sell it."

Recalling what happened to his beloved Ona, Jurgis knows he can't share that point of view. He doesn't tell Marija that he just gave up a foreman's job and $300 "for the satisfaction of knocking down Phil Connor a second time."

In a station-house cell a surge of forgotten emotions causes Jurgis to ponder what has happened to him and his family. "Memories of the old life—his old hopes and his old yearnings, his old dreams of decency and independence!" flash before him, though he has tried to put this all behind.

CHAPTER 28

In the morning a judge frees Jurgis and the other men picked up in the raid. Back at the brothel, Marija tells Jurgis she is addicted to morphine. She also explains how prostitutes are exploited by their bosses: ". . . they let them run up debts, so they can't get away."

Jurgis leaves with Elzbieta's new address—a tenement in the ghetto district, a slum far from Packingtown—but he doesn't go there. Instead, he goes into the same hall he had been in the night before. A political rally, for the Socialists this time, takes up the rest of the chapter.

Jurgis sleeps through a good part of the rally. Finally, a well-dressed young woman nudges him and urges him to listen. The speech itself is wordy, florid, incendiary, but the speaker is electrifying and has the knack of making Jurgis feel as if he has been singled out. We can assume that the emotionalism of the appeal and the cheers of 2000 already-converted Socialists also affect Jurgis.

But it's the message, not the delivery of it, that wins him over. He believes the message because it describes his experiences exactly. And it explains that experience as a universal condition that workers can reverse. Jurgis is that man "whom pain and suffering have made desperate. . . . And to him my words will come like a sudden flash of lightning . . . revealing the way . . . [and] solving all problems. . . . The scales will fall from his eyes, . . . [and] he will leap up with a cry of thankfulness, . . . a free man at last! A man delivered from his self-created slavery!" You put yourself into this trap, he tells Jurgis, but you can get yourself out.

The speech is also a recapitulation of the novel's major themes. Under capitalism, ". . . all the fair and noble impulses of humanity, . . . are shackled and bound in the service of organized and predatory Greed!" In Chicago, "women are . . . driven by hunger to sell their bodies to live." "Homeless and wretched" men, "willing to work and begging for a chance," are "starving." Children are "wearing out their strength and blasting their lives in the effort to earn their bread!" Mothers struggle "to earn enough to feed their little ones!" Old people, "cast off and helpless," await death.

Living off these oppressed people are "the masters of these slaves, who own their toil. . . . They live in palaces, they riot in luxury and extravagance. . . . The whole of society is in their grip, the whole labor of the world lies at their mercy."

What electrifies Jurgis and the others is the glimpse of the future the orator presents. He envisions the oppressed as a mighty giant rising against the oppressors. The audience is that giant in miniature. It comes "to its feet with a yell; . . . And Jurgis is with them, . . . shouting to tear his throat." He sees that he has made peace with his fate, that he had "ceased to hope and to struggle." But no more. The orator has pointed him toward a new goal. Jurgis's whispered

"By God! By God! By God! at the end of the chapter emphasizes his determination to reach that goal.

NOTE: The Russo-Japanese War   During the 1904 presidential election campaign, a war between Russia and Japan was front-page news. The two nations were fighting for control of Manchuria, a region of northeast China. Japan stunned the world by whipping the Russians in spectacular land and sea battles. The orator compares the horrors of war to the sufferings and death that result from the struggle in Chicago between "wage-slaves" and their "masters."

CHAPTER 29

Jurgis's education about socialism—and, Sinclair hoped, his readers' education—begins with this chapter. After the speech, the orator puts Jurgis in touch with Comrade Ostrinski, a Polish tailor who had been jailed in Europe for his politics. Ostrinski takes Jurgis to his apartment, where with his family he ekes out a living as a pants finisher.

Ostrinski's crash course to educate Jurgis begins with an explanation of the competitive wage system. Workers have only their labor to sell, and jobs go to the lowest bidders. So workers are forced by this system to accept wages that they can barely live on. Two great classes are forming: the capitalist class "with its enormous fortunes" and the proletariat—industrial workers "bound into slavery by unseen chains."

The proletariat is the larger group, but it lacks organization and class consciousness. With effort and patience, that organization will come about and in the socialist scheme the workers will then use the vote to take over the government and end private ownership of industry.

Jurgis applies these concepts to the Beef Trust before he beds down for the night on the floor of Ostrinski's kitchen. Now he can begin to understand how the packers used him. He has trouble getting to sleep. He can't get out of his mind a "joyful vision of the people of Packingtown marching in and taking possession of the Union Stockyards!"

CHAPTER 30

Jurgis's political education continues after he lands a job as porter at a hotel owned by a Socialist named Tommy Hinds. Hinds has a cure for every problem, large or small: "Vote the Socialist ticket!"

His hotel is a "very hot-bed of propaganda." Everyone who works there is a Socialist, and the party line is pushed on all the guests—even on the Western cattlemen who stay there.

Jurgis, now living with Elzbieta and her children, becomes an avid reader of tracts and newspapers. He also attends political meetings regularly, where sometimes he hears "speakers of national prominence."

NOTE: Socialists of "National Prominence" Readers in 1906 would have recognized some of the speakers Sinclair describes but doesn't name. Jack London, the "young author," traveled the world and became famous for *The Call of the Wild* (1903), *The Sea Wolf* (1904), and *White Fang* (1905). The "millionaire Socialist" whose magazine had been "driven to Canada" is Gaylord Wilshire—like London, one of Sinclair's friends; he made his fortune selling billboard advertisements. Sinclair even put himself in this chapter as the author of a manifesto that urged socialism on the Chicago unionists who lost the packing-house strike in 1904.

The *Appeal to Reason* is the Socialist weekly that
serialized *The Jungle* before it appeared in book form.
Sinclair's detailed description of its contents reads like
a promotion letter, which he probably meant it to be.
But the description also shows something Sinclair was
at pains to point out—that socialists have a sense of
humor.

It is obvious now that Jurgis has thrown off his
timidity with his chains. He speaks up at a Democratic
rally to say that both major parties buy votes. He'd go
on, but two friends make him sit down. This is a far
cry from the Jurgis we used to know.

CHAPTER 31

The chapter opens with a visit to Marija, whom Jurgis fails to convince to quit prostitution, and ends with
a rousing speech at a Socialist gathering, a rather hap-
hazard and unsatisfying way to end a novel. Sinclair
knew it; in 1909 he called the ending "pitifully inadequate." Later, in his *Autobiography*, he explained: "The
last chapters were not up to standard, because both
my health and my money were gone, and a second
trip to Chicago, which I had hoped to make, was out
of the question."

Excuses aside, probably no other ending would
have satisfied Sinclair's urge to propagandize for socialism in 1905. At heart, he was a pamphleteer.

NOTE: Pamphleteering Pamphleteering—writing short, paperbound books to promote a point of
view in a political or religious controversy—has a long
and noble history. John Milton, the English poet,
wrote several books on divorce, church government,
and press freedom. In the 1770s, pamphlets by

Thomas Paine presented convincing arguments for American independence. A pamphlet was relatively inexpensive and easy to print and often escaped the eyes of government censors. Thus, it was the ideal medium for a writer with a controversial point of view.

Today, we attach the label pamphleteer to writers who promote their ideas with the singlemindedness of the early pamphlet writers. Sinclair is one such writer. In the last chapter, he all but discards his other hats (storyteller, historian, and muckraker) to promote socialism.

The conversation that is at the center of the chapter takes place at the home of a wealthy young social worker. The occasion is a visit from a magazine editor who wants to learn about socialism. The other guests include Jurgis, a "philosophical anarchist" named Nicholas Schliemann, and a Christian socialist named Lucas.

Schliemann and Lucas represent opposite poles of the party. They agree on only two points: 1. Everything needed to produce food, clothing, and shelter—"the necessities of life"—should be publicly owned and managed in a democratic manner. 2. That goal will be achieved only if wage earners are taught to view themselves as a distinct class and to act together politically.

Like the American writer Henry David Thoreau, Schliemann is a rarity: a person who lives his life as an experiment. He lives alone ("No sane man would allow himself to fall in love until after the revolution," he says) on $125 a year, which he earns as a migrant farm laborer each summer.

Once an itinerant evangelist, Lucas grafted social-ism to his religious beliefs and now travels "all over the country, living like the apostles of old, upon hos-pitality, and preaching upon street corners." To him, socialism is an updated version of the teachings of Jesus—"the world's first revolutionist, the true founder of the Socialist movement; a man whose whole being was one flame of hatred for wealth."

Schliemann disagrees. To him, socialism is "a nec-essary step toward a far-distant goal"—an anarchistic society which encourages "the free development of every personality, unrestricted by laws." Schliemann sees religion as a weapon of oppression that "poi-soned the stream of progress at its source." He envi-sions a socialist paradise. The competitive wage sys-tem would be gone, and so would war and its costs. Profits would be gone; goods would be sold at a price equal to the cost of the labor required to make them. Also gone would be the costly wastes of competition: industrial warfare, vice, an expensive legal system, political corruption, the purchase and production of frivolous items, the idle rich. (Everyone would be required to work.) In their place would rise "positive economies of co-operation": shared housekeeping and cooperative cooking, scientific farming, labor-saving machinery. In such a world, Schliemann promises, "anyone would be able to support himself by an hour's work a day."

The novel ends the next day as the Socialists tally up election returns in a meeting hall. The numbers Sinclair gives are accurate; they reflect the unexpect-edly strong showing for the Socialist candidate for president, Eugene V. Debs, in 1904. In the three wards of Packingtown, 6300 men (women couldn't vote in presidential elections then) backed the Socialist ticket. No wonder Boss Scully had been worried during the aldermanic elections!

Jurgis is in the hall listening to party officials announce the returns. A speaker who seems to Jurgis "the very spirit of the revolution" exhorts the crowd to organize and build on the party's gains. With "outraged workingmen" on their side, says the orator, "Chicago will be ours!" (The speech is based on one Sinclair made on election night in 1904.)

It's a curious ending. It holds out hope for future change—but no certainties. And it allows Jurgis to slip out of sight, to become just an anonymous part of the cheering crowd in the hall.

Perhaps that's intentional. It's an axiom of socialism that individuals get their strength as part of the mass. Nonetheless, we want to know more about Jurgis at this point, because we're left with an unfinished portrait of him. He's unhappy living with Elzbieta. She is ill and her boys have picked up some rough habits on the streets. Yet he can always turn from his problems to the Socialist movement—"this great stream"—and to learning. "He was just a hotel porter," Sinclair tells us, "and expected to remain one while he lived; but meantime, in the realm of thought, his life was a perpetual adventure."

By becoming ordinary, our hero becomes something less than a hero. But he has survived. For a wage-slave in Packingtown, that's nothing short of miraculous.

A STEP BEYOND

Tests and Answers

TESTS

Test 1

1. Upton Sinclair   _____
   A. attacks the wage slavery of capitalism
   B. advocates public ownership of the means of production
   C. both A and B

2. Who presents Socialist views?   _____
   A. Jack Duane
   B. Ostrinski
   C. Jokubas Szedvilas

3. Which character is *not* part of Scully's organization?   _____
   A. Freddie Jones
   B. Phil Connor
   C. Bush Harper

4. The wedding of Jurgis and Ona is delayed by the   _____
   A. unexpected difficulties with the immigration authorities
   B. insistence of the older family members that they wait till they can afford the traditional feast
   C. couple's decision to wait till Jurgis has found a job

5. Sinclair depicts corruption in the ____
  A. graft taken by employees of each level
from those below them
  B. collusion between the company that sold
homes to the workers and the owners of the
meat packing plants
  C. deals between the government
inspectors and the plant owners

6. One of the difficulties Jurgis must cope with ____
is
  A. losing his job if he joins the union
  B. reporting for work at seven though
actual killing of the cattle may not start till
the afternoon
  C. Ona's reluctance to return to work after
their child is born

7. Jurgis discovers ____
  A. the Beef Trust is his best hope of getting
and keeping a job
  B. he has outgrown Packingtown and
strives for a more intellectual life
  C. working harder may not, after all, solve
his problems

8. Jurgis turns to drinking ____
  A. to forget Ona's infidelity
  B. when he gets into the habit of accepting
free lunch in the saloon
  C. as a way of overcoming the effects of
working in the fertilizer plant

9. Which statement is *not* true? ____
  A. In jail Jurgis learns Ona has lost her job
  B. Jurgis is sent to jail for almost choking
his wife to death

C. Jurgis curses the society that gives food
and shelter to a prisoner but turns his family
out of their home to freeze and starve

10. Jurgis returns from prison to find   _____
    A. Madame Haupt attending the birth of
       Ona's second child
    B. his family living in the attic of the
       widow's boardinghouse
    C. Connor and his cronies waiting to
       avenge his attack on Connor

11. To what extent might Sinclair be called a disciple of the
    French Naturalist Émile Zola? Cite plot developments,
    imagery, and documentary techniques to support your
    answer.

12. A critic (Alfred Kazin) has called *The Jungle* "the most
    authentic and most powerful of the muckraking nov-
    els." In what way is *The Jungle* a muckraking novel? To
    what does it owe its authenticity and power?

13. Show how Sinclair uses language, plot, characteriza-
    tion, and setting to develop the metaphor of his title.
    Cite specific examples.

14. *The Jungle* is a novel of propaganda. Discuss.

15. Analyze Jurgis's role as a naïf, and show how the role
    helps Sinclair develop his themes.

Test 2

1. Jurgis finds work at a steel mill with the   _____
   help of
   A. a settlement worker
   B. Marija's employer
   C. the steelworker he meets in the police
      station

2. The death of Jurgis's son Antanas is the   ____
   result of
   A. slow starvation
   B. an accident at Mike Scully's dump
   C. his drowning in the street after a heavy
      rain

3. The novel shows Jurgis working in the   ____
   harvester plant and the steel mills, as well
   as in the stockyards, to show he is
   A. caught in a system that uses him and
      discards him at will
   B. representative of all workingmen
   C. both A and B

4. Of whom is it said: "She was one of the   ____
   primitive creatures: like an angleworm,
   which goes on living though cut in half; like
   a hen, which deprived of her chickens one
   by one, will mother the last that is left her"?
   A. Marija
   B. Elzbieta
   C. the widow Jukniene

5. In his summer sojourn in the country, Jurgis   ____
   A. finds there is a stern system in Nature in
      which only the strong survive
   B. feels his former obligations to his family
      in Chicago had condemned him to a life
      of despair
   C. both A and B

6. Which statement is true?   ____
   A. Jurgis is successful as a beggar, but his
      conscience will not permit him to
      support himself this way.
   B. Jurgis is impressed by the sermon of the
      evangelist who provides a warm hall for
      the beggars and unemployed.

C. Jurgis is taken to a mansion on Lake
   Shore Drive by a drunken young man
   he meets.

7. Jurgis's experiences with Jack Duane and   _____
   Mike Scully help convince him that
   A. the world of crime is the surest road to
      success
   B. the alliance between business, politics,
      and crime must be overcome by a radical
      change in society
   C. in politics, an individual is more likely to
      become the "user" than the "used"

8. The brothel scene followed by the scene   _____
   with the Socialist speaker presents
   A. the reason for evil in society and its
      opposite
   B. a symbol of the sickness of society and
      its cure
   C. the contrast between slavery and power

9. The final scenes in the novel depict   _____
   A. the growth of socialism as a means of
      ending the oppression of the workers
   B. the relentless subjugation of an
      individual by powers he cannot control
   C. a dramatic change in Jurgis's
      opportunities

10. According to Sinclair, socialism   _____
    A. can be achieved by unionization of all
       workers
    B. requires a complete restructuring of
       society
    C. can be advanced by paying no more for
       anything "than what it costs to make it"

11. Describe Sinclair's technique of varying the moods and the ways of presenting information, and show how he uses the technique to advance the plot.

12. Discuss the effects of capitalism on the family as they are explored in *The Jungle*.

13. How did Sinclair expect socialism to correct the political and business abuses he describes in the novel? Give specific examples.

14. Discuss Sinclair's use of humor in *The Jungle*, noting instances of irony and comic characterizations.

15. The inability of Old World values to survive in capitalist America is one of the minor themes in the novel. Discuss, with particular reference to Marija's experience.

ANSWERS

Test 1

1. C   2. B   3. A   4. B   5. A   6. B
7. C   8. C   9. B   10. B

11.   Zola saw himself as a kind of scientist, studying the way heredity and environment determined his characters' fates. He didn't create plots, he said; nature did. A person's natural urges and hereditary flaws and strengths dictated his reactions to his environment.

Zola's books were experiments that showed how these forces boxed in his characters. With such a structure, his novels usually ended in despair. (For a more thorough discussion of Zola's technique, see the note on natural selection in Chapter 7. See also the explanation of the Naturalist approach under Themes.)

Sinclair was not a Naturalist, although he adopted several of Zola's techniques. As he said, he tried to put "the content of Shelley in the form of Zola." (The English poet Percy Bysshe Shelly was a romantic revolutionary who advocated radical solutions to social problems in his poems and pamphlets.) Like a scientist conducting an experiment, Sinclair put his subjects—a peasant family—into an alien environment to test their survival skills.

Zola reported his characters' environment in all its sordid detail. So did Sinclair—right down to dead roaches (Chapter 7). Zola detailed his characters' techniques of survival. So did Sinclair, describing, for example, how newsboys learn their jobs (Chapter 12), the eating of frozen garbage (Chapter 21), work in a fertilizer plant (Chapter 13), and life in a brothel (Chapters 27, 28). Zola let chance play a decisive role in his novels. So did Sinclair. The fate of his characters is determined by the weather (Chapter 8), or stalled trolleys (Chapter 15), or the coincidence of Jurgis's walking into a Socialist rally (Chapter 28).

But Sinclair took Zolaism only so far. The unforgiving environment took Jurgis's wife, father, and child, but Jurgis survived. For him, at least, the book ends on a promising note—a very unlikely Zolaist ending. Moreover, Sinclair did not see himself as an impartial scientist. From the dedication ("To the Workingmen of America") to the last page, he is partisan to the worker. Ultimately, *The Jungle* is a piece of propaganda for socialism—a far cry from one of Zola's "experiments."

12. President Theodore Roosevelt gave the label "muckraker" to those writers who specialized in exposing business abuses and political corruption. Most of these writers put their charges in magazine articles and nonfiction books, but a few, like Sinclair, incorporated them into fiction.

The Jungle contains well-researched exposés of child labor (Chapters 6, 7, 12), rigged horse races (Chapter 25), political corruption (Chapters 9, 25, and elsewhere), sexual harrassment (Chapters 10, 15), dangerous working conditions (Chapters 7, 9, 11, 12, 21, 23, and elsewhere), unsanitary housing (Chapters 2, 7), unfair labor practices (Chapters 8,

20, and elsewhere), real estate fraud (Chapters 6, 10), spoiled and adulterated food (Chapters 3, 9, 11, 14), and many other abuses. The authenticity of the charges is backed up by a wealth of detail, including a footnote on U.S. regulations (Chapter 9).

Sinclair has a knack of making us share his outrage. He related his exposés to people we care about, so that we are outraged when we read of diseased meat or unpaved roads killing children (Chapters 13, 21) or when crooked judges give Jurgis unjust sentences (Chapters 17, 25) or when Dede Antanas is refused a job because of his age (Chapter 5) and is then finally killed by the job he does get (Chapter 7).

Furthermore, Sinclair's exposés—especially of the meat-packing industry and working conditions there (Chapter 9)—contain so much visceral detail that they knock the wind out of us. (For more on muckraking, see The Author and His Times and the chapter-by-chapter discussions.)

13.   Greed and ruthless competition—two conditions of unbridled capitalism, Sinclair contends—have turned Chicago into a jungle. "Take or be taken," "kill or be killed" are guiding rules.

Sinclair uses similes and metaphors to drive this point home. For example, in Chapter 15, Ona has the "eye of a hunted animal," and Jurgis pants hoarsely, "like a wounded bull." Jurgis "sprang" into a room to find Connor, "his prey," "this great beast." He fights "like a tiger," and like a jungle cat sinks "his teeth into the man's cheek." Such images crop up throughout the novel.

Characters act like animals, and two even have nick-names that suggest the wild. "Bush" Harper and "Buck" Halloran are two evil political operators no one should turn his back on. Indeed, "Bush" Harper, the last time we see him (Chapter 26), is passing off his planned theft of Jurgis's savings as an act of friendship.

The setting is a natural expression of the novel's title. Sinclair sums it up (Chapter 17): Chicago was "a city in which justice and honor, women's bodies and men's souls, were for sale in the marketplace, and human beings writhed and fought and fell upon each other like wolves in a pit, in which lusts were raging fires, and men were fuel, and humanity was festering and stewing and wallowing in its own corruption." It was, Sinclair says, a "wild beast tangle."

Sinclair structures the plot to give Jurgis (and us) a guided tour of this jungle. Jurgis learns that Brown's meat-packing plant is "a seething cauldron of jealousies and hatreds; there was no loyalty or decency anywhere about it, there was no place in it where a man counted for anything against a dollar." As a consumer, Jurgis learns about fraud—by real estate agents, manufacturers of roach powder, trolley car companies, saloon keepers. He sees the jungle as a member of Chicago's criminal underworld, too. (His partner, Jack Duane, says of life there: "It is a case of us or the other fellow.") In these realms and others, "nothing counted but brutal might, an order devised by those who possessed it for the subjugation of those who did not" (Chapter 24).

14. *The Jungle* is designed to sell its author's solution to society's problems. That solution, socialism, is not presented until the last four chapters, where a number of speeches, dialogues, and conversations spell out its promise. The first 27 chapters represent Sinclair's description of the problem: a world turned into a jungle by the ruthless competition and greed built into the capitalist system.

In many ways, these chapters are the most important. Before we're willing to accept, or even consider, Sinclair's solution, we must accept his definition of the problem. He must prove to us that capitalism debases every institution and person it touches. Plot, characterization, setting, language—Sinclair uses all these tools to persuade us that his vision is correct. (See the answer to the previous question for examples.)

Unfortunately, Sinclair's solution does not have the force, in fictional terms, that his description of the problem has. The reason: His argument, so full of concrete detail, becomes unfocused and abstract when he introduces socialism. Thus, the last four chapters miss their mark. "I aimed at the public's heart," Sinclair said, "and by accident I hit it in the stomach."

As propaganda for socialism, *The Jungle* fails. But as a description of the effects of an oppressive economic system and an industrial nightmare, the book is a resounding success.

15. Sinclair sets up Jurgis as a naïf in Chapter 2. (See the discussion of Chapter 2.) Jurgis brushes off "stories about the breaking down of men," for "he was young, and a giant besides. . . . He could not even imagine how it would feel to be beaten." The men who hear him size him up as a country bumpkin. "It is plain that you have come from the country, and from very far in the country," they say.

The rest of the novel describes Jurgis's education about the real world. Again and again, he or people he loves are cheated, "used up" by work, killed, injured, sexually abused, and exploited in other ways. Along the way, Sinclair develops his themes: about the recklessness of capitalism, the exploitation of children, the brutalization of the worker, and so on.

With all his strength, Jurgis is powerless to prevent any of the catastrophes that befall his family. The man who begins the novel as a defender of "rugged individualism" ends up as an advocate of collective action, of democratic revolution led by the working class.

Test 2

1. A **2.** C **3.** C **4.** B **5.** B **6.** C
7. B **8.** B **9.** A **10.** B

11. The first 27 chapters embody a long downhill slide into disillusionment and despair. But along the way, the characters rest on plateaus of optimism, taking time to catch their breaths and hoping for better luck. For many of the characters that lucky break never comes; for Jurgis it doesn't occur until Chapter 28, when he discovers socialism.

The alternation of up-and-down moods is evident in almost every chapter, beginning with the wedding feast in Chapter 1. The chapter opens in a rush of excitement, with Marija riding herd on the guests and with the musicians playing frenziedly. The mood sags when Marija teaches the musicians a sad song and Dede Antanas gives a lugubrious speech. A lighthearted speech by Jokubas has the guests smiling again and picks up the pace; the dancing that follows is joyful. But the happy mood begins to fade when it comes time to ante up money for the wedding feast. By the end, drunkenness, fatigue, and the approach of another working day have sunk the party into a sea of gloom.

Similar mood swings mark nearly every chapter—so much so that a happy mood is usually a clue that disaster is near. Jurgis's job in the harvester plant (Chapter 20) encourages him "to pick up heart again and make plans." A paragraph later, he is laid off. The next time that he begins to "make plans and dream dreams" (Chapter 21), he returns home to find little Antanas dead.

Sinclair varies the way he presents information, too. For the most part he summarizes the action. Other times he dramatizes it, with actual scenes and dialogue. In many muckraking passages (Chapter 9, e.g.) he simply describes what he sees, like a nonfiction writer. At the end of the novel, he turns to speeches (Chapters 28, 31), dialogues (Chapter 31), and lectures (Chapter 29) to explain social-ism.

The technique of varying moods and ways of presenting information adds suspense to the plot and helps hold our attention. Some readers complain that he overuses sum-mary narrative. Yet it is hard to imagine how he could cover the ground that he does without relying so heavily on this technique.

12.   The families as a whole in *The Jungle* can't withstand the effects of greed and competition any more than their individual members can. Jurgis's extended family disinte-grates before our eyes. The "system" claims the lives of two adults and three children. Another member—Jonas—dis-appears. Marija becomes a prostitute, Elzbieta a sick woman whose children pick up "wild and unruly" ways on the streets.

Throughout the novel, Sinclair makes it plain that family life for the wage-slave is incompatible with a brutal eco-nomic system. In Chapter 10, at Antanas's birth, Jurgis becomes "irrevocably a family man." Yet the little time he has to see his baby makes him feel the "chains" about him more than ever. Only when he is out of work with an injury (Chapters 11, 21) can he enjoy his child.

Nor can husbands and wives enjoy each other. When-ever Ona and Jurgis "talked they had only their worries to talk of—truly it was hard, in such a life, to keep any senti-ment alive" (Chapter 12). They are torn apart by the pres-sures on Ona to become a boss's mistress. Ironically, for the sake of the family, she gives in to the man's demands.

Nicholas Schliemann, the ex-professor of philosophy, believes that "no sane man would allow himself to fall in love until after the revolution" (Chapter 31). The battering taken by Jurgis's extended family shows why. With a fam-ily, a worker is especially vulnerable to exploitation. Only when he is left on his own, without wife and child, does Jurgis feel free enough to reject a job offer in the country.

13.   In a socialist economy, private individuals would no longer own the "means of production." Factories, mines, mills, farms—all would be owned by the public and run democratically. The immediate effect in Chicago would be that the workers would take over the packing plants from the Durhams, Browns, and Joneses. Public ownership would do away with the profit motive. The economy would no longer be a place where people could satisfy their greed. With greed and profit eliminated, people would not feel compelled to take advantage of each other, to "take or be taken."

The workers who ran the enterprises after the revolution would also presumably have no incentive to sell adulterated or spoiled meat or otherwise to cheat customers. Nor would anyone have an incentive to exploit labor—to "use up" workers the way profit-oriented capitalists did.

The competitive wage system would vanish, and wages would rise. Working conditions would improve, because workers would no longer have to settle for any job. They could pick and choose, and most would choose not to work in dangerous places. But rather than pay extremely high wages to lure workers, it would be cheaper to modernize packing plants and hazardous factories.

Government would be free of corruption. Sinclair traces political corruption under capitalism to greedy businessmen trying to get the power of the government on their side. Since there would be no reward for greed under a socialist system, no one would have any reason to "buy" government officials. True democracy would return; cooperation would replace competition; and the jungle would become a Garden of Eden.

14.   Some people think that irony is the highest form of humor because it is the most subtle; it says one thing and means another. Sinclair uses irony throughout *The Jungle*.

Some examples: In Chapter 3, Jurgis says, "I'm glad I'm not a hog," after watching hogs led to slaughter—yet Sinclair, with an allegory, has already suggested that he is. In Chapter 5, Sinclair parodies advertisements by having Jurgis accept their outrageous promises literally, as if they had been prepared by people who wanted to "see that his health and happiness were provided for," In Chapter 27, Sinclair mocks a Republican senator's pitch for protective tariffs by calling them "an ingenious device whereby the working-man permitted the manufacturer to charge him higher prices." Naming a bulldog after a war hero—and thus mocking the war hero—is another form of irony (Chapter 24).

Several of Sinclair's characterizations are comic. The elfin Tamoszius is funny in Chapter 1, funnier after he falls in love in Chapter 8 with his opposite, Marija, who "could have picked him up and carried him off under one arm." The greasy Madame Haupt, the midwife, is a grotesque who makes us laugh nervously in Chapter 19. Sinclair uses Freddie Jones, the teenage son of a major meat packer, to satirize the lopsided values of the rich. Tommy Finnergan, in Chapter 8, seems to serve no other purpose but comic relief. He's a harmless nut who tries to interest Jurgis in the "shperrits"—higher intelligences that "may be operatin' upon ye." Of course, there are forces working on Jurgis— the inexorable forces of unbridled capitalism. If Finnergan is in touch with those, he doesn't show it.

15. Many of the immigrants in the novel are determined to maintain the values they brought with them. Marija is seen trying to uphold them on the first page—seeing "that all things went in due form and after the best home traditions." By the last chapter, she has renounced those traditions and accepted life as a prostitute and dope addict. She has "come to regard things from the business point of view."

Marija's renunciation of the community values she learned in Lithuania isn't complete. She uses her money to support Elzbieta's family—what's left of it. Yet she has become a criminal. She is following a pattern described in chapter 1, when freeloaders break the "compact" of the *veselija* and refuse to contribute. "Since they had come to the new country, all this was changing; it seemed as if there must be some subtle poison in the air that one breathed here."

Greed and competition force even the young to adapt or perish. Elzbieta, who begged neighbors for the money to give Kristoforas a proper burial and Ona a requiem mass, must send Nikalojus and Vilimas into the streets to sell newspapers. She can't prevent them from "taking on the tone of the new environment"—swearing, smoking, gambling (Chapter 13). By Chapter 31 they are living at home, thanks to Marija's largess, but they are "very much the worse for their life upon the streets." In an economic jungle, where the rule is "Take or be taken," the Old World communal values cannot thrive.

Term Paper Ideas

A Critique of Capitalism

1. Describe the way Sinclair develops his theme that the American economic system at the turn of the century was an efficient, impersonal "slaughtering machine" that sacrificed its workers.

2. Explain how Jurgis's many jobs support Sinclair's contention that it is the economic system, not just a particular industry, that needs fixing.

3. How do children serve Sinclair's purpose as muckraker and propagandist? Discuss children of the rich as well as of the poor.

4. One of the tenets of capitalism is that competition benefits the consumer. How does *The Jungle* demonstrate the opposite—that competition, combined with greed, is actually disadvantageous to the consumer?

5. Companies need profits to grow—to develop new products, build new plants, open new markets. How do events in *The Jungle* allow Sinclair to argue that profits can be evil, as well?

Socialism

1. Analyze the action of the novel in terms of conflict between two classes: the proletariat and the capitalists.

2. Compare and contrast Schliemann's and Lucas's views of religion and socialism.

3. Describe Sinclair's opinion of unions. How does this opinion support his thesis that socialism is the worker's best hope?

Technique

1. Show how Sinclair uses symbols, metaphors, and similes to develop his theme that greed and ruthless competition have made turn-of-the-century America a brutal jungle.

2. Discuss Sinclair's use of summary narrative in *The Jungle*. Where is it the most effective? Where is it the least?

3. Describe Sinclair's use of sensory imagery—word pictures that appeal to our senses—in an attempt to put us into his characters' world.

4. Sinclair's talents as a researcher are evident on nearly every page of *The Jungle*. Explain.

5. Illustrate Sinclair's technique of setting off developing characters by pairing them with their opposites. Use examples of couples and others who may be opposite in such ways as physical appearance, experience, and social class.

Characters

1. Discuss how Sinclair uses Mike Scully to show that greed corrupts the political system.

2. Jurgis begins the novel as an advocate of individual action. He ends it as an advocate of collective action. Discuss, and then give three examples of how he supports each position.

3. Although sick at the end, Elzbieta has a knack for survival that few of the other characters have. Analyze that knack, referring to particular incidents and descriptions of her.

Miscellaneous

1.   The naturalist Charles Darwin taught that the survival of a species depends on its ability to adapt to its environment. Apply this theory to Sinclair's turn-of-the-century Chicago, and to the characters of Ona and Marija.

2.   Discuss turn-of-the-century Chicago as a desirable setting for a novel of propaganda such as *The Jungle*.

3.   Discuss Sinclair's treatment of blacks, comparing it to his treatment of other powerless groups, such as Lithuanian and Polish immigrants and women.

4.   *The Jungle* suggests that immigrants are more easily exploited than native-born Americans in a capitalist society. Discuss.

5.   Discuss Sinclair's criticism of advertising, and show how he uses advertisements to advance his plot.

6.   The house that the family struggles to keep and that it finally loses is one of the novel's central symbols. Discuss.

Further Reading

CRITICAL WORKS

Becker, George J. "Upton Sinclair: Quixote in a Flivver." *College English 21* (1959): 133–40.

Blinderman, Abraham, ed. *Critics on Upton Sinclair.* Coral Gables, FL: University of Miami Press, 1975.

Bloodworth, William A., Jr. *Upton Sinclair.* Boston: Twayne, 1977.

Brooks, Van Wyck. *The Confident Years.* New York: Dutton, 1953.

Dell, Floyd. *Upton Sinclair: A Study in Social Protest.* New York: George H. Doran, 1927.

Dickstein, Morris. "Introduction"; *The Jungle.* New York: Bantam Books, 1981.

Downs, Robert B. "Afterword"; *The Jungle.* New York: New American Library, 1960.

Harris, Leon. *Upton Sinclair: American Rebel.* New York: Thomas Y. Crowell, 1975.

Hicks, Granville. "The Survival of Upton Sinclair." *College English 4* (1943): 213–20.

Kazin, Alfred. *On Native Grounds.* New York: Reynal & Hitchcock, 1942.

Knight, Grant C. *The Strenuous Age in American Literature.* Chapel Hill: University of North Carolina Press, 1954.

Rideout, Walter B. *The Radical Novel in the United States, 1900–1954.* New York: Hill and Wang, 1956.

Van Doren, Carl. *Contemporary American Novelists, 1900–1920.* New York: Macmillan, 1922.

Yoder, Jon A. *Upton Sinclair.* New York: Frederick Ungar, 1975.

AUTHOR'S OTHER WORKS

Sinclair wrote scores of books, including 42 novels, 25 works of nonfiction, more than 10 plays, two volumes of autobiography, and other books. The following is a selection of Sinclair's works.

Fiction:

Love's Pilgrimage,   1911
King Coal,   1917
Jimmie Higgins,   1919
Oil!,   1927
Boston,   1928
World's End,   1940
Between Two Worlds,   1941
The Return of Lanny Budd,   1953
Affectionately Eve,   1961

Nonfiction:

The Industrial Republic,   1907
The Profits of Religion,   1918
The Goslings,   1924
A Personal Jesus,   1952

Autobiography:

American Outpost,   1932
The Autobiography of Upton Sinclair,   1962

Glossary

Adulterate To make something—food, cement, drugs, water—impure by adding inferior elements. The meat packers in *The Jungle* shortchanged their customers by adding potato flour to their sausages.

Anarchist Someone like the character Nicholas Schliemann (Chapter 31), who believes that full social and political liberty depends on abolition of governmental restraints. Socialism, in Schliemann's view, was a means to that end.

Capitalism An economic system based on private ownership of the means of production, and a market economy regulated largely by the supply of goods and services and the demand for them. In Sinclair's day, capitalism was closer to the pure form, laissez-faire, which rejected a government role in the economy as interference.

Class consciousness The perception by wage earners that they belong to a class (the proletariat) with common grievances and goals. According to socialists, this perception is a prerequisite to political organization and revolution.

Competitive wage system A system of compensation in which workers compete with one another to "sell" their labor. The system ensures that unskilled jobs will usually go to those workers willing to accept the lowest wages.

Corruption The act of making someone dishonest or disloyal, usually through bribery.

Darwinism The theory of Charles Darwin (1809–82), the English naturalist, that holds that all species continually struggle to survive. The species with the best chance, he felt, are those most able to adapt to their environments. Species that are the least fit fail to reproduce, and die out. Sinclair believed in Darwin's theory and continually alludes to it in *The Jungle* to describe his characters' struggles. (See especially Chapter 7.)

Evangelist   A Christian preacher—often a wandering or irregular one—who tries to pass on the teachings of Jesus, which appear mainly in the first four books of the New Testament, called the gospels, or evangels. Lucas, the Christian socialist in Chapter 31, had at one time been an itinerant evangelist.

Graft   Dishonest gain, especially through abuse of one's position in business or government.

Muckrakers   The name President Theodore Roosevelt gave writers who attacked corrupt politicians and business practices during the first decade of this century. Among the leading muckrakers were Ida Tarbell, Lincoln Steffens, and Upton Sinclair. Their works helped raise public support for reform.

Oligarchy   A system of government in which a privileged minority without popular support holds the reins of power.

Plutocracy   Rule of the wealthy, or the wealthy ruling class itself.

Proletariat   The working class, made up mainly of people who have nothing to sell except their labor. In ancient Rome the word referred to the class of people without property. The socialist philosopher Karl Marx popularized the term in *The Communist Manifesto* in 1848.

Settlement worker   An early social worker who lived among immigrants and other poor people in urban slums. One of the first settlement workers was Jane Addams (1860–1935), who in 1889 co-founded a social settlement called Hull House in Chicago. Sinclair tried to convert her to socialism when he visited Chicago to research *The Jungle*.

Socialism   A body of ideas that blames many of society's ills on competition for profit. Socialists want to substitute cooperation for competition. They want the government to control the enterprises that produce goods and services and to direct those enterprises toward socially responsible projects, not just profitable ones. *Democratic socialists,* such as Sinclair, believe that voters in free elections should decide the extent of the government's role in the economy.

Trust A corporation or group of corporations that dominates an industry, squeezing out competition and keeping prices high. The Sherman Act of 1890 outlawed trusts, but they continued to exist well into the 20th century.

Wage slaves Wage earners who are bound to their work by "unseen chains" (i.e., their desperation). The competitive wage system kept them in poverty and enabled their employers to exploit them. *The Jungle* is largely an exposé of the way these "working poor" were treated during the early years of this century.

The Critics

Jurgis' Conversion

The conversion of Jurgis to socialism, at the end of the book, was really impossible after his soul had been "murdered," as one was told, and the story of his life was quite unreal when, after the death of his wife and his child, he became a hobo, a scab, and a crook. He was as unreal, in fact, as his friend Duane, the fancy man, or the young millionaire who invites him to his house in Chicago, a figure of pure melodrama in which Sinclair reverted to his early pulp-writing. . . . Sinclair's characters, as a rule, were puppets.

> —Van Wyck Brooks, *The Confident Years*, 1953.

Jurgis does not have enough inner life to make his final conversion credible. Even in its powerful early chapters, the book demands a surprisingly narrow range of emotion from the reader. The more the characters are trapped by the system, they are transformed from agents to mere victims, and the principal feeling asked of us is pity—one of the most dehumanizing of all emotions, since it turns people into objects of our compassion rather than subjects in their own right.

This somewhat stunted humanity prevents *The Jungle* from being one of the truly great novels of city life, however accurate its social and economic framework may be.

> —Morris Dickstein, "Introduction," to *The Jungle*, 1981.

The "conversion" pattern of *The Jungle* has been attacked as permitting too easy a dramatic solution; however . . . it should be noted that in *The Jungle* Sinclair carefully prepares such an outcome by conducting Jurgis through all the circles of the workers' inferno and by attempting to show that

no other savior except Socialism exists. Perhaps a
more valid objection to the book is Sinclair's failure
to realize his characters as "living" persons. . . .
They gradually lose their individuality. . . . Yet
paradoxically, the force and passion of the book
are such that they finally do come to stand for the
masses themselves, for all the faceless ones to
whom things are done. Hardly individuals, they
nevertheless collectively achieve symbolic status.
> —Walter B. Rideout, *The Radical Novel*
> *in the United States, 1900–1954,*
> 1956.

The Use of Propaganda

The question is . . . whether the agitprop [agi-
tation and propaganda for socialism] in *The Jungle*
damaged this novel as form and as narrative, and
the answer must be affirmative. The declamatory
final chapter . . . is uplifting but it is also artificial,
an arbitrary re-channelling of the narrative flow, a
piece of rhetoric instead of a logical continuation of
the story, and throughout most of the book the
woes piled upon Jurgis and his family are so concentrated as to assault the imagination. However,
this damage is too slight to spoil the complete
effect. *The Jungle,* with an argument now out of
date, remains one of the most heartrending ac-
counts in fiction of what ignorant and helpless
human beings have endured.
> —Grant C. Knight, *The Strenuous Age*
> *in American Literature,* 1954.

A Study of Economics

There are two general approaches which Sinclair makes in all [his] novels. One is a close, doc-
umented study of the working of some specific
economic mechanism; the other is a charge of general conspiracy for the maintenance and extension
of privilege on the part of the beneficiaries of the
system. *The Jungle* is relatively successful because it

leans heavily on the former technique, though the
charge of conspiracy is implicit throughout.
—George J. Becker, "Upton Sinclair:
Quixote in a Flivver," *College English 21*, 1959.

Sinclair's Vision

"Nothing about [Sinclair] has done more to
make him an arresting novelist than his conviction
that mankind has not yet reached its peak, as the
pessimists think; and that the current stage of civilization, with all that is unendurable about it,
need last no longer than till the moment when
mankind determines that it need no longer en-
dure. He speaks as a Socialist who has dug up a
multitude of economic facts and can present them
with appalling force; he speaks as a poet sustained
by visions and generous hopes.
—Carl Van Doren, *Contemporary
American Novelists, 1900–1920*,
1922.

LaVergne, TN USA
10 November 2010
204357LV00005B/93/A